Samuel Henshall

The Saxon and English Languages Reciprocally Illustrative of each other

Samuel Henshall

The Saxon and English Languages Reciprocally Illustrative of each other

ISBN/EAN: 9783337209766

Printed in Europe, USA, Canada, Australia, Japan

Cover: Foto ©Thomas Meinert / pixelio.de

More available books at **www.hansebooks.com**

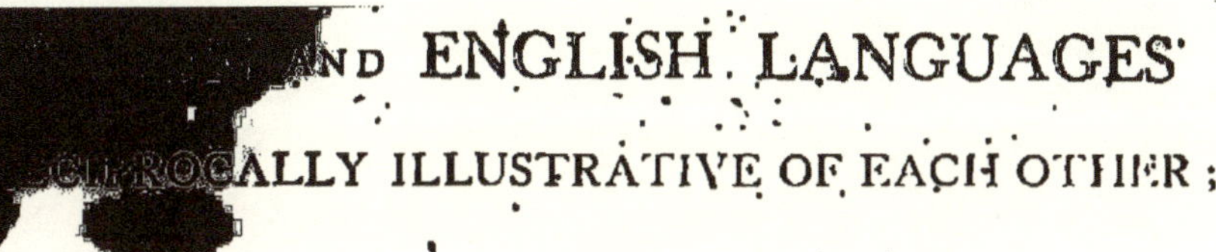

…AND ENGLISH LANGUAGES

…ALLY ILLUSTRATIVE OF EACH OTHER;

THE

IMPRACTICABILITY OF ACQUIRING

AN ACCURATE KNOWLEDGE OF SAXON LITERATURE,

THROUGH THE MEDIUM OF LATIN PHRASEOLOGY,

EXEMPLIFIED IN THE ERRORS OF

HICKES, WILKINS, GIBSON, AND OTHER SCHOLARS,

AND A

NEW MODE SUGGESTED OF RADICALLY STUDYING
THE SAXON AND ENGLISH LANGUAGES,

BY SAMUEL HENSHALL, M. A.

FELLOW OF BRAZEN-NOSE COLLEGE, OXFORD, AND AUTHOR OF SPECIMENS AND PARTS OF THE HISTORY OF SOUTH-BRITAIN.

READING I TEACH.
rædende ic teace.

BEDA.

LONDON:

PRINTED FOR THE AUTHOR;

AND SOLD BY

NICOL, PALL-MALL; PAYNE, MEWS-GATE; WHITE, FLEET-STREET; RIVINGTONS, ST. PAUL'S CHURCH-YARD; SEWELL, CORNHILL; HANWELL AND PARKER, OXFORD; LUNN, CAMBRIDGE; AND CLARKE, MANCHESTER.

MDCCXCVIII.

TO

THOMAS ASTLE, Esq. F.R.S. AND S.A.

TRUSTEE OF THE BRITISH MUSEUM, SOC ANTIQ. CASSELL. SOD, &c.

RESPECTED SIR,

THE Favours received, and the Information derived, by my free Admiſſion to your invaluable Library, demand my earlieſt Acknowlegements, not only on the Principle of Juſtice, but from my grateful Conſciouſneſs of the high Obligation conferred upon me. No ſooner had my SPECIMENS of the HISTORY OF SOUTH-BRITAIN appeared, than you became its avowed Patron, invited me to your Houſe, permitted me the unlimited Peruſal of your ANCIENT DOCUMENTS, SAXON MANUSCRIPTS, and ANSTIS'S NOBLE COLLECTION of EXTRACTS and AUTHORITIES, and generouſly allowed me to tranſcribe whatever could illuſtrate the antient State of the Britiſh Realm. Not reſting here, you have entruſted valuable Volumes to my Cuſtody, referred me to the beſt Sources of Information, and introduced me to Gentlemen and Scholars, the Keepers of our national Records, to which I have had eaſy Acceſs. When the next Number of my Hiſtory appears, the Advantages derived from ſuch Opportunities

tunities will be manifested to the Public; and the numerous References to the Manuscripts in your Possession, will best evince my Opinion of their Worth, and Sense of your Kindness. In the mean Time, though you are fully convinced that the Books of DOMESDAY have been my more immediate Study, permit me to present you with the First-fruits of my Proficiency in Saxon Learning, a Language essentially necessary for understanding many Parts of this AUTOGRAPH, till I can with Prudence pursue my grand Undertaking.

I am, respected Sir,

Your truly obliged

and sincere humble Servant,

LONDON, AUG. 10, 1798.

SAMUEL HENSHALL.

THE

SAXON AND ENGLISH

LANGUAGES, &c.

THE Study of the Anglo-Saxon Language has certainly engaged the attention of able Scholars and learned Divines. The ancient Records of this realm have been collected with laudable assiduity, many of them have been printed with a Version, and more liberally translated. To assert that no correct ideas can be collected from the laborious exertions of a Hickes, a Gibson, or a Wilkins; to affirm that their Latin interpretations are of little authority, unintelligible, and delusory; argues certainly a daring Challenger, or a Champion conscious of the merits of his cause, and therefore not easily intimidated.

The present investigator relies little on his own knowledge, but is confident in the errors of his opponents; he is better acquainted with antient Latin Records than Saxon Documents, but having been compelled, in the course of his investigations, to consult the Thesaurus of Hickes, the Leges Saxonicæ of Wilkins, &c. and finding it impossible to form any certain inference from their Latin jargon, he was necessitated to examine the Original, in its vernacular idiom. Of the result of this investigation let others judge; but before condemnation is passed, let the evidence be candidly weighed by the judgment of a discerning jury. For this purpose we shall submit the Original in Saxon Characters, with the Version and Interpretation of the Editor's on one page; the Original, in Roman Characters, with the literal verbatim Rendering, in italics, on the other, that a just [a] verdict of their merits may be returned by an honest and impartial juryman.

To trifle away time is not the object of our researches. We shall therefore select a most curious Record for observation, the very first that the learned Hickes has inserted in his Dissertatio Epistolaris, and which he considers a valuable [b] document, conveying important information. This reports the Saxon process in an Assize, or the manner of holding a grand Court of Judicature for a County. It has deservedly occupied his peculiar attention and engaged his particular comment. We cannot therefore be accused of acting uncandidly in our selection, since we begin with one of our ablest scholars, take the first occurring Record in this part of his publication, and which he has certainly endeavoured to illustrate with precision. Far is it from our intention likewise to detract from the merit of such men, they have laboured for the great advantage of posterity; but our immediate object is to prove, that the mode of study adopted by them was insufficient to produce a correct knowledge of the Idioms of the Anglo-saxonic Language,

[a] Vere-dictum.

[b] Inter hæc autem merito *primum locum vendicat* Causæ sive Litis cujusdam in Comitiis, &c. Differt. Epist. p. 2.

which

which has little ſimilarity with a Latin Conſtruction, but is ſo really and truly our old Engliſh Tongue, that Lord Lyttleton ſo denominates a Saxon Proclamation in the reign of Henry the third, and Warton's Early Extracts in his Hiſtory of Engliſh Poetry, are as pure Saxon, as can be produced at that æra. In the courſe of this inveſtigation, Specimens will be given, to illuſtrate, and ſupport, this aſſertion; for as Scholars, at this period, were generally Prieſts accuſtomed to the Romiſh Ritual, we muſt neceſſarily expect a mixture of Latin Phraſeology in all their Compoſitions.

A SAXON

A SAXON MANUSCRIPT, transcribed from the Harleian Collection, with the Latin Version of HICKES.—Thesaur. Vol. 2. Dissert. Epist. p. 2.

Her swutelað on ðissum gewrite þ an scir-gemot sæt æt Ægelnoðes-stane be Cnutes dæge Cinges: Ðær sæt on Æðelstan b. Ranig Ealdorman. ⁊ Edwine þæs ealdormannes. ⁊ Leofwine Wulsiges sunu. ⁊ Ðurcil Hwita. ⁊ Tofig Pruda com þær on þæs Cinges ærende. ⁊ þær wæs Bryning scir-gerefa. ⁊ Ægelweard æt Frome. ⁊ Leofwine æt Frome. ⁊ Godric æt Stoce ⁊ ealle þa þegnas on Hereford-scire: Ða com þær farende to þam gemote Edwine Enneawnes sunu. ⁊ spæc þær on his agene modor æfter sumon dæle Landes. þ wes Weolintun. ⁊ Cyrdesleah. Ða acsode þe

VERSIO HICKESIANA.

In hoc scripto ostenditur, Comitatus conventum quendam habitum fuisse Ægelnothes-stane Rege Canuto regnante. In quo quidem conventu considebant Æthelstanus Episcopus & Ranigus Comes & Edwinus Comitis & Leofwinus Wulsigei filius. Eò etiam convenerunt ad negotia regis gerenda Thurcilus cui Albus [a], & Tosigus cui comptus, cognomen erat, cum Bryningo vice-comite, Ægelweardo Fromensi, Goodrico Stocensi, & omnibus pagi Herefordensis liberis hominibus. Tum ad conventum profectus Edwinus Ennawnes filius, agebat contra matrem de quorundam prædiorum jure, quibus nomina erant Weolintun, & Cradesleah. Controversiâ autem

[a] The original is wight—a wise man—a read man—a Counsellor, for all Thanes were not Witena. There is not the least authority for the insertion of Cognomen. See Dissertation on Ranks and Customs.

The SAME MANUSCRIPT; the SAXON in ROMAN, the ENGLISH in ITALIC CHARACTERS.

Here [a] *settleth on this Writ, that one Shiremote sat at*
Her swutelath on thissum Gewrite, that an Scir-gemot sæt æt
Ælnoth's Stone, being Cnutes Day King. There satten Ethel-
Ægelnothes-stane, be Cnutes Dæge Cinges. Thær sæton Æthel-
stan Bishop, and Raney Elderman, and Edwin this Elderman's,
stan B. and Ranig Ealdorman, and Edwine thæs Ealdormannes
and Leofwin Wulfig's Son, and Thurchill Wight, and [b] *Tosig*
and Leofwine Wulfiges Sunu, and Thurchil Hwita and Tosig
Proud came there on this King's Errand, and there was Bruning
Pruda com thær on thæs Cinges Ærende; and thær wæs Bruning
Shire-reeve and Egelward at Frome, and Leofwin at Frome,
Scir-gereva and Ægelweard æt Frome, and Leofwine æt Frome,
and Godric at Stoke, and all the Thanes in Herefordshire.
and Godric æt Stoce, and ealle tha Thegnas on Hereford-scire.
Then came there fore-hand to that Mote Edwin Enneawnes
Tha com thær fa-rende to tham [c] Gemote Edwine Enneawnes
Son, and spake there on his own Mother, after some Deal of
Sunu, and spæc thær on his agene Modor, æfter sumon Dæle
Lands, that was Wellington and Curdsley. Then asked the
Landes, thæt was Weolnitun and Curdesleah. Tha ascode the

[a] Hence our modern Settlement, and it is settled, determined.

[b] Hickes's Version "Tosig cui comptus cognomen erat," destroys the idea intended to be conveyed by the Original, of the attendance of the King's Justiciary; and how he could omit such a circumstance, and so render the passage, is astonishing.

[c] The Saxon *ge* prefixed, is almost constantly to be left out in modern English.—Mote was a County-meeting or Assize—hence moot-point—for the decision of such Court, dedisse ei Motam de Hereford cum toto Castello, Rym. Fæd. vol. 1. p. 8.

biscop. hwa sceolde and-swerian for his modor: Ða and-sweorode Þurcil Hwita. ⁊ sæde ꝥ he sceolde. gif he þa talu cuðe. Þa he þa talu nane cuðe: Ða sceawode man þreo þegnas of þam gemote þær ðær heo wæs. ⁊ þæt wæs æt Fæliglæh. þæt wæs æt Fæliglæh. þæt wæs Leofwine æt Frome. ⁊ Ægelsig þe Reada. ⁊ Þinsig Stægðman. ⁊ þa þa heo to hire comon þa acsodon heo hwylce talu heo hæfde ymbe þa land þe hire sunu æfter spæc: Ða sæde heo ꝥ heo nan land hæfde þe him aht to gebyrede. ⁊ gebealh heo swiðe eorlice wið hire sunu. ⁊ gecleopade ða Leoflæde hire magan to hire Þurcilles wif. ⁊ beforan heom to hire þus cwæð. her sit Leoflæde min mæge þe ic geann ægðer ge mines landes. ge mines goldes ge ræglæs. ge reafes. ge ealles þe ic ah æfter minon dæge. ⁊ heo syððan to þam þegnon

ab illo motâ, rogavit Episcopus, quisnam responsurus esset pro matre Edwini, cui statim Thurcilus Albus se pro illa responsurum ait, si causam, unde actio [b] descenderet, sciret, cujus nullam esse sciebat. Tum conspecti erant in conventu tres liberi homines, nempe Leofwinus Fromensis, Ægelsigus Rufus, & Thinsigus Stægthmannus, qui erant è vico Fæligleahensi, ubi mater Edwini habitabat. Hi à curia mandati erant, ut ad eam profecti rogarent, de jure quod haberet ad terras, de quibus filius ejus controversiam movisset. His autem illa respondens dixit se nullas terras habere, quas ille [c] aliquo juris prætextu vendicare posset, & dein heroica quadam indignatione in suum filium vehementer excandescens, & Leofledam propinquam suam Thurcili uxorem advocans, sic coram illis prope se sedentem eam allocuta est. Ecce Leofledam propinquam meam, cui Ego cum prædia mea, tum aurum, tum etiam vestes & in-

[b] If any man can form an idea, of the original sense intended to be conveyed, from such a version, or any precise idea at all, I am much deceived.

[c] How simple, clear and definite the word "birth" when compared with this.

dumenta.

Bishop, who should [d] ante-swear for his Mother. Then ante-
Biccop, hwa sceolde and-swerian for his Modor. Then and-
sweareth Thurcil Wight and said that he should, if he that Tale
sweorote Thurcill Hwita and sæde that he sceolde, gif he tha Talu
[d] *couth, tho he that Tale none couth. Then sheweth man three*
cuðe, tha he tha Talu nane cuðe. Tha sceowode man thres
Thanes of that Mote there [e] there [f] hoo was, and that was at
Thegnas of tham gemote thær thær heo wæs, and thæt wæs æt
Faleylae. That was Leofswin at Frome and Alsig the Red,
Fæliglæh. Thæt wæs Leofswine æt Frome and Ægelsig the Reada,
and Thinsig Stedman, and they then hie to their [f] Common; then
and Thinsig Stægdman, and tha tha heo to hire Comon, tha
asked they what Tale hoo had about that Land, that her
acsothon hoo hwulce Tale heo hæfde ymbe tha Land the hire
Son after spoke. Then said hoo that hoo no Land had, that
Sunu æfter spæc. Tha sæde heo that heo nan Land hæfde, the
he ought to birth; and bawled hoo with Earl's Wrath her
him aht to gebyrede, and gebealh heo [g] swithe eorlice [h] w..th hire
Son & yclept there Leoflæde her Kinswoman to her Thurkill's
Sunu & gecleopade tha Leoflæde hire Magan to hire Thurcilles
Wife, and before them to her thus quoth. Here sit Leofled my
Wif, and beforan heom to hire thus cwæth. Her sit Leoflæde min

[d] Ante-swear—the Latin ante against. [d] Couth—knew.

[e] Modern where.

[f] Hoo—she—Hoo-Justice—Female Justice. Lancashire Dialect, by Tim Bobbin, Esq; a Mr. Collier, of Rochdale; a Work of great original humour, and of infinite advantage to the Student of Saxon Literature, relative to Spelling.

[f] Common Court of their District.

[g] This word our Saxon Lexicographers have always rendered strenue, vehementèr, magnoperè, but it certainly is synonimous and of equal power with our modern *with*, as a radical uncompounded word, as *Mihtum swith*—Might with, or with Might. *Swith-fearmian* Lyes crudescere with Ferment, &c.

[h] The MS. much injured, non sine Mendis plurimis, vid. Hickes, but probably wræth.

cwæþ. doð þegnlice. ⁊ wel abeodað mine ærende to þam gemote beforan eallum þam godan mannum. ⁊ cyðaþ heom hwæm ic mines landes geunnen habbe. ⁊ ealre minre æhte. ⁊ minan agenan sunu næfre nan þing. ⁊ biddað heom beon þisses to gewitnesse: And heo þa swæ dydon. ridon to þam gemote. ⁊ cyðdon eallon þam godan mannum hwæt heo on heom geled hæfde. Ða astod Ðurcil hwita up on þam gemote. ⁊ bæd ealle þa þægnas syllan his wife þa landes clæne. þe hire mage hire ge-uðe. ⁊ heo swa dydon. ⁊ Ðurcill rad ða to

dumenta, tum denique omnia, quæ habeo, me mortuâ, fruenda concedo. His dictis, dein liberos homines à curia missos sic adfatur. Eja agite, ut liberos homines decet, & diligenter perferte mandata mea ad Curiam, fideliter declarantes coram omnibus probis hominibus, cui terras meas omnes, & universa bona eâ intentione dedi, ut filium meum exhæredem facerem, & rogate eos, ut huic donationi testes esse velint. Illi protinus, quod petierat, præstiterunt. Equis enim conscensis, ad conventum remeant, & coram probis hominibus universis, quod se præsentibus Enneawne se descendens protulerat, declaraverunt. Quibus quidem declaratis, surgens, in [d] foro Thurcilus Albus ab omnibus liberis hominibus postulabat, ut uxori suæ terras a lite immunes adjudicarent, quas illi propinqua ejus donaverat. Hi vero ita fecerunt, prout rogaverat Thurcilus, qui statim consenti-

[d] By such versions all historical accuracy has been destroyed; where can be found a term corresponding with "coram probis hominibus universis, et ab omnibus liberis Hominibus in Foro—the Original only specifies the Thanes assembled in the County Court, our present Grand Jury.

entibus

Kinswoman that I've given after yea my Lands, yea my
Maege the ic geann ægther ge mines Landes, ge mines
Golds, yea Pells, yea Ruffs, yea all that I have after my
Goldes, ge Pæglæs ge Reafes ge calles the ic ah æfter minon
Days, & hoo fiththen to them Thanes quoth. Do Thanelike,
Dæge & heo fyththan to tham Thegnon cweth. Doth Thegnlice,
and well bid mine Errand to that Mote before all
& wel abeodath mine ærende to tham Gemote beforan callum
them good men, and couth them whom I my Lands
tham godam mannum & [i] cythath heom hwæm ic mines Landes
given have, and all me [k] *ought and mine own* [l] *Son*
geunnen habbe, & ealre minre æhte, & minan agenan Sunu
never none Thing, and biddeth them be on this to Witness, and
næfre nan Thing & biddath heom beon thisse to gewitnesse &
they then so didden, ridden to their Mote, and coudden all
heo tha swæ dydon, ridon to tham Gemote & cyddon callon
them good men what hoo on them laid had. Then stood
tham godan mannum hwæt heo on heom geled hæfde. Tha astood
Turchill Wight up in that Mote and bid all the Thanes
Thurcil hwita up on tham Gemote & bæd calle tha Thægnas
shall his Wife the Lands clean, that her Kins-woman her giveth,
syllan his Wife tha Landes clæne, the hire Mæge hire geuthe
and they so didden, and Turkhill rid then to St. Æthelbert's
& heo swa dydon, & Turcill rad tha to see Æthelberhtes

[i] Couth opposite to uncouth—I am surprized with an uncouth fear—Shakespear—Vid. Skinner.—Uncouth in arms yclad—Spenser.—Unknown, consequently *couth* make them know.

[k] Ought—modern, to me owed.

[l] Alfred's grandfather had entailed many estates on the Spear-half, and had excited probably no little animosity and jealousy among the Spindle-half; hence such maternal affection.—See hereafter.

D *Mingle*

ſc̄e Æþelberhtes mynſtre be ealles þes folces leafe. ⁊ ge-witneſſe. ⁊ let ſettan on ane Criſtes boc.

entibus univerſis, qui conventui intereſſent, cum omnium teſtimoniis, equo conſcenſo, ad Sancti Æthelberhti monaſterium tendit, ad quod profectus, quod actum erat in quendam Evangeliorum codicem referri curavit.

Minster by all those Folks Leave and Witness and [m] *leet setten*
Mynstre be alles thæs Folcs Leafe & gewitnesse & let settan
in One Christ's Book.
on ane Cristes Boc.

We entertain little doubt that English Scholars will imbibe more correct ideas of the Original from our homely Version, than from the Latin of Hickes; and the Historian and Lawyer have better notions of Courts of Judicature at this æra. To comment at large on this Record is not our immediate object, for we reserve it for discussion in that Dissertation of our History, where we shall consider Customs as the Common Law of the Realm. The next Specimen we shall exhibit is a Charter of the Conqueror's, published likewise in the Thesaurus, with an antient Latin Version.

[m] Let—permitted.

CHARTER

CHARTA WILHELMI REGIS CONQUESTORIS

DE SACA ET SOCNA.

Willm̄ King gret mine biscopes ⁊ mina eorles. ⁊ ealle mine þegnas frencisce ⁊ englisce on þan scýran ƿer scs̄ Augustinus herd land inne freondlice. ⁊ ic cýðe eow þ͞ ic habbe ge-unnan Gode and scē Augustine. ⁊ þam hirede þe þerto hýreð. þ͞ hieo bien heore sace ƿeorðe ⁊ heora socna. ⁊ griðbrýces. ⁊ ham-socna. ⁊ forstalles ⁊ infangenes þeofes. ⁊ flemene-ferminðe ofer heora agne men binnan burgh and butan. tolles and teames. on strande ⁊ on streame. ⁊ ofer sƿa fele þegna sƿa ic heom to ge-leten habbe. ⁊ ic nelle þat anig man anig þing þeor on-teo butan heom. ⁊ here ƿicneres þe hƿo hit beo-tecen ƿillan. for þam þe ic hebbe for-gifen gode. ⁊ scē Augustine þas gerihte mine saple to alýsednesse. ealsƿa Eadƿord king min meg ær erfde. ⁊ ic nelle geþafian þæt

Ego Wilhelmus rex saluto omnes meos epos & comites, & omnes meos optimates francigenas & anglicos, in illis comitatibus ubi Sanctus Augustinus terram habet. Notum vobis esse volo me annuisse Sancto Augustino suæque congregationi, ut habeant suum Sake & Sockne, & pacis fracturam & pugnam in domo factam, & viæ assaltus & fures in terra sua captos, & latronum susceptionem super suos proprios homines intra civitatem, & extra * ··· in litoribus & in marinis fluctibus, quod Anglice dicitur teames & super omnes allodiarios suos. Et ego nolo consentire, ut aliquis de aliqua re se intromittat exceptis semetipsis, & suis præpositis, quibus ipsi commiserunt, vel committere voluerunt. Concedo enim istas rectitudines Deo & S. Augustino, meæ animæ ad redemptionem,

sicut

CHARTER OF WILLIAM THE CONQUEROR.

William King greet my Bishops and mine Earls and all
Willm King gret mine Biscopes & mina Eorles and calle
my Thanes french and english in them shire where St. Au-
mine thegnas frencisc & engliose on than scyran wes Stus Au-
gustine haveth land in [a] friendlike and I [b] couth you, that I
gustinus hefd land inne freondlice and ic cythe eow, that ic
have given God and St. Augustine and the Herd that
hæbbe ge-unnan Gode & Sce Augustine and tham hirede the
thereto heireth that they be their Sac worthy and their Soc
therto hyneth that hæo bien heore Sace weorthe and heora Socne
and [c] agreed-break and homesteal and foresteal and within-fanging-
and Grithbryces and hamsocna and forstalles and infangenes
thief and fleemen [d] frims over their own men within Borough
theofes and flemene-fermthe ofer heora agene men binnan burgh
and without.
and butan.

[e] *Tolles and theam*
Tolles and teames
On Strand and in Stream
On Strande and on Streame

and over such fealty thanes such I them to let have and I
and ofer swa fele thegna swa ic heom to ge-leten habbe and Ic

[a] Synonimous perhaps with modern Franchise.

[b] Contrary to uncouth, make you know.

[c] *Agreed*-break—what was settled or established by the grand Council of the Nobility—*Grith*, Agreement. Chaucer.

[d] Lincolnshire Dialect—Frims—folk—from ƿpembe—a stranger—hence—from.

[e] Doubtless the Poetry of the age.

ænig man þis abrecan be minan freondscipe. God eoƿ gehelð. amen.

ſicut Edwardus meus conſanguineus, & ſui anteceſſores reges fecerunt. Et ego nolo conſentire, ut aliquis iſtud frangat, qui de mea amicitia curet. Valete.

[f] *will that any man any thing thereunto* [g] *but them and their*
nelle that anig man anig thing theor on-teo butan heom, and here
Vicars the who it take will, for that that I have
Vicneres the hwo hit beo-tecen willan, for tham the Ic habbe
fore-given Gode and St. Augustine, thus to right my soul to
for-gifen Gode and See Augustine, thas gerihte minne sawle to
loosednesſ all so Edward King my Kinsman eer feed and I nill
alysednesſ ealswa Eadword King min Meg ær efde and ic nelle
suffer that any man this break by mine friendship. God
gethasian thæt ænig man this abrecan be minan frendscipe. God
you hold. Amen.
cow geheld. Amen.

Since the learning of Hickes has hitherto never been questioned, since [h] Dr. White Kennet states his "Instructions of Grammar to be methodical and accurate," since Bishop Nicholson reports his "Book as discovering an accuracy in this language beyond the attainments of any that had gone before him in this study;" since Gibson, Smith, and Thwaites have extolled his ability in England; Grævius, Wormius, and the Leipsic Acta Eruditorum on the Continent, we judge it expedient to give other Specimens of his inaccurate Versions, and unfaithful Translations.

[f] Nill, not will. Vid. Chaucer passim.

[g] See Tooke's Diversions of Purley.

[h] Vide Testimonia Auctorum apud Hickes Thesaur. Vol. 1st. *Gibson*—circa singulas pæne voces hæsi, veritus ne iis subesset idiotismi nescio quid, mihi adhuc non quidem plane incogniti, sed tamen haud satis bene intellecti. Verum cum re prope desperatâ totum Consilium tantum non abjecissem, omne hoc incommodum opportunè sustulit *Clarus Georgius Hickesius*—*Smith*—Subsidia & quasi Manu-ductiones, quæ viam ad abditissima Penetralia (Linguæ Anglo-Saxonicæ addiscendæ) apertam, planam ac facilem muniunt ex Docti Somneri Dictionario & Docti Hickesii Grammaticâ suppeditantur.—Thwaites—Hickesi literaruræ hujus omnis Instauratori maximo—*Grævius*—Vir pereruditus—*Wormius*—Legi iterumque perlegi—*Acta eruditorum* Vir hic doctissimus.——

EXCERPTA E PSEUDO EVANGELIO NICODEMI.

Hick. Gram. Anglo-Sax. p. 72.

Ða cwæþ sco helle to Satane. La ðu ealdor ealre forspylle-dnysse. ⁊ la ðu ordfruma ealra yfela. ⁊ la ðu feder ealra flymena. ⁊ la ðu þe ealdor wære ealle deaþes. ⁊ la ordfruma ealre modignysse. for hwig ge-dyrstlæhtest ðu ðe þ ðu þ geþanc on þ Iudeisce folc asendest þ hig ðyrne Hælend ahengon. ⁊ ðu him nænne gylt on ne oncneowe. ⁊ ðu nu þurh þ treow ⁊ þurh ða rode hæfst ealle þyne blysse forspylled.

Tum inquit Morta [Hecate] ad Satanam : ô tu princeps perditionis ! ô auctor omnium malorum ! ô profugorum [apostatarum] omnium pater ! ô qui fuisti princeps omnis interitûs ! ô omnis ambitionis auctor ! cur præsumebas indere in mentes Judæorum, ut Jesum, quem sciebas esse innocentem, crucifigerent, quando quidem per [a] ligneam illam crucem tuam, omnem delectationem perdidisti. Evang. Nicod. p. 17. §. xxix.

[a] Ligneam,—a *wooden* Translation indeed.

LEGES

EXTRACTS FROM THE FALSE GOSPEL OF NICODEMUS.

Then quoth ſhe Hell to Satan Lo thou calder Earle of *ſore-*

Tha cwæth ſeo Helle to Satane. La thu caldor earle for-

ſpoiledneſs, and lo thou [a] *earth-former* of *all evil, and lo thou*

ſpylldnyſſe, and la thu ordfruma ealra yſela and la thu

father of *all ſleemen, and lo thou thee* [b] *the that, thou that* [c] *Think*

fæder ealra ſlymena and la thu the the that, thu that gethanc

in that Judaiſh folk haſt ſent, that they this Healing one high-hang,

on that Judeiſce folc aſendeſt, that hig thyſne Hælend ahengon,

that thou him none guilt on never once knew, and thou now

that thu him nænne gylt on ne oncneowe, and thu nu

thorough that true one, *and thorough that* [d] *Rood haveſt all thine*

thurh that tryw, and thurh that Rode hæfſt ealle thyne

Bliſs fore-ſpoiled.

blyſſe foreſpylled.

That an accurate Inveſtigator can never be ſatisfied with the Verſions of Hickes, we preſume is clearly eſtabliſhed. The Author ſelected for our farther animadverſions is David Wilkins, the laborious Editor of the Concilia and Leges Saxonicæ. We ſhall ſelect a Section from the Laws of the Confeſſour, which we defy any Scholar or Lawyer to comprehend or interpret, from his pretended Tranſlation. We wiſh not hence to infer that our Conjectures or Rendering are uniformly right, for Saxon Records want the penetration and judgment, that Bentley diſplayed in Greek and Roman Literature, to purify their Text; we pretend to prove, however, that our predeceſſors have been groſsly wrong, and that many of their errors have proceeded from their purſuing the ſtudy of Anglo-Saxon Learning through the medium of the Latin Language.

[a] Earth, the Source of every thing, the general Mother, and Cauſe of Life.

[b] This. [c] Think—ſynonimous with modern thought. [d] Synonimous with Croſs.

LEGES EDWEARDI REGIS.

Wilkins Versio. p. 49. §. 2.

Be ðone þe oþrum rihtes ƿýrnþ.

Eac ƿe cƿædon hƿæs se þýrþe ƿære ðe oþrum rihtes ƿýrnde. aþor oþþe on boclande. oþþe on folclande. hƿonne he him rihte ƿorhte beforan þæm gerefan : Gif he þonne nan rihte næfde. ne on bocolande ne on folclande. ꝥ se ƿære þe rihtes *a* ƿýrnde scýldig xxx scill. ƿið ðone Cýning : *b* Æt oþrum cýrre eac sƿa : æt ðriddan cýrre. Cýninges oferhýrnýsse. ꝥ is cxx scill. buton he ær gesƿice.

De eo qui alteri jus denegat.

Item diximus, quod dignum esset alteri jus denegare, sive in possessione propria, sive in fundo populari, quando ei jus datur coram Præfecto. Si tunc nullum jus habeat nec in possessione propria, neque in fundo populari, sit ille qui jus denegat reus xxx solidorum apud Regem ; altera vice eodem modo ; tertia vice contumaciæ erga Regem, hoc est, cxx solidorum, nisi se prius excuset.

LEGES

LAWS OF EDWARD.

Wilkins. p. 49. §. 2.

Of them that other rights warneth.
Be thone the othrum rihtes wyrnth.

Eke we woud, whoso he worthy were, that other Rights
Eac we cwædon hwæs se wyrthe wære the othrum rihtes
warneth, either oth' on Bookland, oth' on Folkland, whence
wyrnde, athor oththe on Bockland, oththe on Folcland, hwonne
he him right works before those Reeves. If he then none
he him rihte worhte beforan thæm Gerevan. Gif he thonne nan
right not have, nay on Bookland, nay on Folkland, that he were
rihte næfde, ne on Boclande, ne on Folclande, that se wære
the Rights worthy [a] sinneth 30 Shill with the King: At
the Rihtes [b] wyrd scyldig xxx scill with thone Cuning: Æt
other [c] Court eke so; at third Court, Kings overhighness,
othrum Curre eac swa; æt thriddan Curre, Cuninges oferhyrnesse,
that is 120 shillings.
that is cxx Scil.

[a] In the various readings of the Laws of this æra we find scynning and scyldig, in different MS.

[b] Lambard thus, pẏrð, certainly more intelligible than pẏrnðe.

[c] Courts were held every fortnight at this æra

LAWS

LEGES ÆLFREDI.

Wilkins Versio. p. 43. §. 37.

Be Boclande.

Se mon seþe boclande hæbbe. ⁊ him his magas læfden þonne setton ƿe ꝥ he hit ne moste syllan of his mægburge gifðær bið geƿrit. oþþe geƿitnysse. ꝥ hit þæra manna forbod ƿære ðe hit on fruman gestrindon. ⁊ ðara ðe hit him sealdon. ꝥ he sƿa ne mote. ⁊ ꝥ ðonne on Cyninges. ge on Biscepes geƿitnysse gerecce beforan his magum.

Si quis terram hæreditariam habeat, quam Parentes ejus ipsi reliquerunt, tunc statuimus, ut eam non vendat a cognatis hæredibus suis, si adsit scriptura vel testis, quod illi viro prohibitum sit, qui eam ab initio acquisivit, & illi qui eam vendidit, ut ita facere nequeat, & hoc tunc in Regis vel in Episcopi testimonio recitetur coram cognatis suis.

LAWS OF ALFRED.

Wilkins. p. 43. §. 37.

Of Bookland.

If man be that [a] *Bookland have, and him his* [b] *Elders left,*
Se mon ſe the Bockland hæbbe, and him his yldran læfden,
then ſet we, that he it not might ſell off his [c] *Kinſbrother,*
thonne ſetton we, that he hit ne moſte ſyllan of his Mægburge,
if there beeth Writ, oth' Witneſs that it there man
gif thær bith gewrit, oththe gewitneſſe that hit thæra manna
forbad were, that it in firming reſtrained (they) and there that
forbod were, the hit on fruman geſtrindon and thara the
it him [d] *ſealed, that he ſo not might and that then in Kings*
hit him ſealdon, that he ſwa ne mote and that thonne on Cuninges
yea in Biſhops Witneſs be read before his Kinsfolk.
ge on Biſceopes gewitnyſſe [e] geredde beforan his Magum.

[a] Bookland—Entered in one Chriſt's Book.

[b] ẏlbpan Textus Roffenſis Wylkins magaꝑ.

[c] The Spear-half, not the Spindle-half. See this illuſtrated when we examine Alfred's Will.

[d] Sealed in a Charter or Book.

[e] Very probably geredde for gerecce.

PÆNITENTIALE DOMINI ECGBERTI ARCH. EBOR.

Concilia Magnæ Brit. a Davide Wilkins, S. T. P. p. 138.

Gif hƿylc cristen man his agen bearn. oþþe his nehstan mæg ƿiþ anigum ƿurþe sylle. næbbe he nanne gemanan mid cristenum mannum ær he hine alysed hæbbe of ðam þeoƿdome. gif he þonne hine begytan ne mæge. dæle sƿa mycel feoh for hyne sƿa he ær mid him nam. ⁊ alyse oþerne of ðeoƿdome. ⁊ freoge ðone. ⁊ fæste seofon ƿucan on hlafe ⁊ on ƿætere. ⁊ gif he ðær gestreones næbbe ꝥ he alysan mæge. fæste ðonne eahta ⁊ tƿentig ƿucena on hlafe ⁊ on ƿætere.

Si quis chriſtianus infantem ſuum vel proximi ſui pro aliquo pretio vendiderit, non habeat conſortium aliquod cum chriſtianis, antequam eum e ſervitute redemerit; ſi autem ipſum obtinere nequeat, tradat tantum pecuniae, quantum prius per ipſum acceperat, et redimat eum e ſervitute, ac liberet illum, et jejunet ſeptem ſeptimanas in pane et aqua: et ſi facultates non habeat, ut eum redimere poſſit, jejunet octo et viginti hebdomadas in pane et aqua.

PENETENTIAL OF ECBERT ARCHBISHOP OF YORK.

David Wilkins. p. 138.

If ilk Chriſtian man his own Barn, oth' his nigheſt
Gif hwulc Criſten man his agen bearn, oththe his nehſtan
Kinſmans, with any [a]*Worth ſell, not have he no Communion*
mæg, with anigum wurthe ſylle, næbbe he nanne gemanan
with Chriſtian men, e'er he them looſed have of their
mid Criſtenum mannum, ær he hine alyſed hæbbe of tham
thraldom, if he then them get not may, deal ſo mickle
theowdome, gif he thonne hine begytan ne mæge, dæle ſwa mycel
fee for them, ſo he e'er with them [b]*nimmed, and looſe others of*
feoh for hyne, ſwa he ær mid him nam, and alyſe otherne of
thraldom, and free thence, and faſt ſeven Weeks on Loaf
theowdome, and freoge thone, and fæſte ſeofon Wucan on hlafe
and on Water, and if he this ſtrength not have, that he looſe
and on Wætere, and gif he thæs geſtreones næbbe, that he alyſan
may, faſt then eight and twenty weeks on Loaf and on
mæge, fæſte thonne eahta and twentig wucena on hlafe and on
Water.
Waetere.

[a] Synonimous with price.

[b] Nimmed his purſe.—Shakeſpear—Merry Wives of Windſor.

LEGES INÆ.

Wilkins. Concil. p. 59. §. 6.

Be gefeohtum.

Gif hwa gefeohte on cyninges huse. sy he scyldig ealles his yrfes. ⁊ sy on cyninges dome. hwæþer he life age ðe nage: Gif hwa on mynster gefeohte. hund twelti g scillinges. gebete. Gif hwa on ealdormannes huse gefeohte. oþþe on oþres geþungenes witan. sixtig scillinges gebete he. ⁊ oþer syxtig scillinges gesylle to wite: Gif he ðonne on gafolgyldan huse oþþe on geburres gefeohte. ð rittig scillinges to wite gesylle. ⁊ dæm gebure syx scillinges: And ðeah hit sy on middan felda gefohten. hund twelftig scillinges to wite sy agyfen: Gif ðonne on gebeorcipe hi geciden. ⁊ oþer heora mid geþylde hit forbere, gesylle se oþer ð rittig scillinges to wite.

De pugnis. Cap. 6.

Si quis in regis domo pugnet, perdat omnem ſuam haereditatem, et in regis ſit arbitrio, poſſideat vitam an non poſſideat. Si quis in templo pugnet, centum viginti ſolidis mulctetur. Si quis in ſenatoris domo pugnet, vel in alterius illuſtris ſapientis, ſexaginta ſolidis mulctetur, et alios ſexaginta ſolidos ſolvat poenae loco. Si autem in tributarii domo vel coloni pugnet, triginta ſolidos poenae loco ſolvat, et colono ſex ſolidos. Et licet in medio camipi pugnatum ſit, centum viginti ſolidi poenae loco ſolvantur. Si autem in convivio rixati ſint, et unus horum patienter id ſuſtineat, ſolvat alius triginta ſolidos poenae loco.

Be

LAWS OF INA.

Of Fights.

If [a] *wha fight in King's House, be he slighted all his*
Gif hwa gefeohte on Cunninges Huse, sy he scyldig ealles his
[b] *Reeves, and be in King's Doom, whether he* [c] *Life have the*
yrfes and sy on Cynninges Dome, hwæther he life age the
no. If wha in Minster fight, hundred twenty shillings
nage. Gif hwa on Mynster gefeohte hund tweltig scillinges
give boot. If wha in Alderman's House fight, oth' in
gebete. Gif hwa on Ealdormannes Huse gefeohte oththe on
other [d] *Thanes, a Wight, sixty Shillings give boot he, and other*
othres Gethungenes, Witan sixtig Scillinges gebete he, and other
sixty Shillings shall to Wight. If he then in Gable-geld
syxtig Scillinges gesylle to [e] Wite. Gif he thonne on gafoldgyldan
House, oth' in Burgesses, fight, thirty Shillings to Wight
Huse, oththe on Gebures, gefeohte, thrittig Scillinges to Wite
shall, and that Borough six Shillings. And tho' it be in
gesylle, and thaem Gebure syx Scillinges. And theah hit sy on
mid-field fought, hundred twenty Shillings to Wight be
midden feldda gefohten, hund twelftig Scillinges to Wite sy
given. If then in Borough-ship they chiden, and either of them
agyfen. Gif thonne in Gebeorscipe hi geciden and other heora
with with-hold it forbear, shall the other thirty Shillings to
mid gethylde hit forbere, gesylle se other thrittig Scillinges to
Wight.
Wite.

[a] Wha wants me.—Edinburgh Language.

[b] Reeves, synonimous with Rolls—reef the Sails—all his chartered Lands.

[c] Whether he be a Lord or not, hlaꝼoꝛð—Life—Source.

[d] Some Thanes not Wights.

[e] The Lord, who has the Court of Suit and Service, Fines and Forfeitures, or Sac and Soc.

Be ðam ðe heora ȝewitnýſſe beforan biſceope ȝeleoȝað.

De iis quorum teſtes coram epiſcopo mentiti ſunt. Cap. 13.

VII. Gif hwa beforan biſceope hiſ ȝewitnýſſe. ⁊ hiſ wed aleoȝe. ȝebete mid hund tweftiȝ ſcillinȝeſ.

VII. Si alicujus teſtis vel * vas coram epiſcopo mentiatur, compenſet centum viginti ſolidis.

CHRONICON SAXONICUM.

Anno 1137. Gibſon. p. 239.

I ne canne. ⁊ ne mai tellen alle þe wunder. ne alle þe pines ꝥ hi diden wrecce men on þis land. ⁊ ꝥ laſtede þa xix. wintre wile Stephne was king. ⁊ æure it was uuerſe ⁊ uuerſe. Þi læiden gæildes on þe tunes æureū wile. ⁊ clepeden it tenſerie. Þa þe wrecce men ne hadden nan more to giuen. þa ræueden hi and brenden alle þe tunes. ꝥ wel þu mihtes faren all adæis fare ſculdeſt þu neure finden man in tune ſittende, ne land tiled. Þa was corn dære. ⁊ flec. ⁊ cæſe. ⁊ butere. for nan ne wæs o þe land. Wrecce men ſturuen of hungær. ſume ieden

Non autem poſſibile eſt mihi numerare omnia vulnera, omneſque calamitates, quibus afflixerunt miſeros incolas hujus terræ: hoc vero duravit xix. annos, quibus Stephanus fuit Rex, & quotidie deteriore erant conditione. Impoſuerunt tributa oppidis valde frequenter, & illud vocarunt ...... cumque miſeri homines non haberent quicquam amplius quod darent, vaſtarunt & incenderunt omnia oppida; adeo ut poſſes inter diei conficere, nec tamen reperire quemvis hominem in oppido viventem, aut terram cultam. Hinc fuit frumentum carum, & caro, & caſeus,

* What is Vas?

§. 7. *If wha before Biſhop, his Witneſs, and his Wed,*
Gif hwa beforan Biſceope, his Gewitneſs and his Wed
cauſe to lye, give boot with hundred twenty Shillings.
aleoge gebete mid hund twelftig Scillinges.

Any Scholar muſt certainly be convinced of the Inaccuracies of Wilkins, and the impoſſibility of underſtanding the Original from his pretended Tranſlations. The next Extract we ſhall ſelect from the Saxon Chronicle; which has been edited by the learned Gibſon with greater care and fidelity, than we have met with in our reſearches; but ſtill we attempt to prove, even from this beſt Specimen, that the Latin Language cannot convey ideas equally accurate or correct, as may be acquired through the medium of Engliſh Phraſeology.

SAXON CHRONICLE.

I nay can and nay may tell all the Wounds nor all the
I ne canne and ne mai tellen alle the Wundes ne alle the
Pains, that they did wretched men in this Land, and that laſted
Pines, that hi diden wrecce men on this Land, and that laſtede
the 19 Winters, while Stephen was king, and ever it was worſe
tha 19 Wintre, wile Stephne was king, and ævre it was werſe
and worſe. They laid Gelt on the Towns every while, and
and werſe. Hi laiden gæildes on the Tunes æureu wile, and
yclept it [a] *tenth-penny.* [b] *Then the wretched men not had any*
clepeden it tenſeprie. Tha the wrecce men ne hadden nan
more to give, then raviſhed they and burnt all the Towns, that
more to given, tha ræveden hi and brendon alle the Tunes, that

[a] Gibſon ſays "quæ ſit hujus vocabuli ſignificatio videant alii," but every perſon converſant in ancient Records, where there are frequent contractions, knows that tenſepic would be tenſepennic, and collateral hiſtorical authority juſtifies our interpretation.

[b] Synonimous to modern when.

on ælmes þe ƿaren sum ƿile rice men. sum flugen ut of lande. Ƿes næure ᵹæt mare ƿreccehed on land. ne næure heðen men ƿerse ne diden þan hi diden. for ouer siðon ne for-baren hi nouþer circe. ne cyrceiærd. oc nam al þe ᵹod ꝥ þar inne ƿas. ⁊ brenden syðen þe cyrce ⁊ alteᵹædere.

& butyrum, quippe nihil eorum fuit in hac terra. Pauperes peribant fame: nonnulli oſtiatim victum petebant, qui fuerant olim divites; & aliqui terram reliquerunt. Nunquam adhuc erant majores calamitates in hac terra, neque unquam pagni plus mali quam hi fecerunt; tandem enim neque pepercerunt Eccleſiæ, neque cœmiterio, ſed eripuerunt quicquid boni inibi fuit, tuncque ignes admoverunt Eccleſiæ, & rebus quæ ſupereſſent.

well thou mightest [c] *far on all a day, sore shouldest thou ever find*
wel thu mihtes faren all adæis, fare sculdest thu neure finden
man in town sitting, or land tilled. Then was corn dear and
man in tune sittende, ne land tiled. Tha was corn dære and
flesh and cheese and butter, for none nay was in the land. Wretched
flec and cæse and butere, for nan ne wæs o the land. Wrecce
men starven of hunger, some [d] *fedden on alms that were somewhile*
men sturven of hunger, sume jeden on ælmes the weren sum wile
rich men, some flewn out of the land. Was never yet more
rice men, sum flugen ut of lande. Wæs næure gæt mare
wretchedness in land, nor ever heathen men worse nay did, than
wreccehed on land, ne neure hethen men werse ne diden, than
they did, for ever siththence not forborne they neither Church,
hi diden, for over sithon ne for-baren hi nouther Circe,
nor Church-yard, but nimmed all the goods that therein was, and
ne Cyrcejærd, oc nam al the god that thar inne was, and
burnt siththence the Church and altogether.
brenden sythen the cyrce and altegædre.

To prove that Saxon Literature has not been cultivated with greater attention, or success, at a subsequent period; we shall exhibit the Conclusion of Alfred's Will, published by the University of Oxford, with the Annototions and Version of Manning, the Editor of Lye's Saxon Dictionary. And here, we cannot but lament, that the Corrector of the Press should have confounded the Unity of this valuable Document, by printing the Saxon Introduction, in the Register of the Abbey of New-minster, as the Will of the amiable and benevolent Alfred, and confounding the reader by a double preamble, in direct contradiction to the Copy transmitted. As a *literal* English Translation is here attempted, we shall add the Latin Version as a Note, to shew that this Record has been studied through the medium of the Latin Language.

[c] Farr-on—advance. [d] Probably an error, j for f.

EXTRACTS FROM ALFRED'S WILL,

In Bibliotheca Aſtleianâ, p. 24.

ORIGINAL.

⁊ ic bidde on godes naman. ⁊ on his haligra. ꝥ minra maga nan. ne yrfeweardna ne gesпence nan. nenig cyrelif þara þe ic foregeald. ⁊ me west-seaxena witan to rihte gerehton þæt ic hi mot lætan swa freo swa þeowe swaðer ic wille. ac ic for godes lufan. ⁊ for minre saple þearfe. wylle ꝥ hy syn heora freolses wyrðe. ⁊ hyra cyres. ⁊ ic on godes lifiendes naman beode þæt hy nan man ne brocie. ne mid feos manuge. ne mid nænigum þingum. ꝥ hy ne motan ceosan swylcne mann swylce hy swyllan.

⁊ ic wylle þæt man agyfe þam hiwum æt domra hamme hyra land bec. ⁊ hyra freols swylce hand to ceosenne sylce him leofast sy. for me. ⁊ for æl-

3

LITERAL ENGLISH TRANSLATION OF THE EDITOR.

And I beſeech, in God's name, and in his Saints', that of my Relations none, nor of my heirs none do obſtruct, none of the freedom of thoſe that I have redeemed. And for me the Weſt-Saxon Nobles as lawful have pronounced that I them may leave either free or bond whether I will. But I, for God's love, and for my Soul's advantage, will that they be of their freedom Maſters, and of their Will, and I, in God the living's name intreat that them no man do not diſturb, neither by Money-exaction, nor by no manner of means, that they may not chuſe ſuch Man as they will.

And I will that they reſtore to the families at Domerham their Land-Deeds, and their free liberty ſuch perſon to chuſe, as to them moſt agreeable may be;

for

EXTRACTS from ALFRED'S WILL, in the Possession of T. ASTLE, Esq; with a literal verbatim Rendering.

And I bid in God's Name, and in his holy ones, that my
And ic bidde on Godes Naman, and on his haligra, that minra
Megs none no reeveeward not squench none, nor any Court-leave,
maga nan ne urfeweardа ne geswence nan, nænig Curelif,
there that I fore-sealed, and me West-saxon Wights to right
thara the ic forescald, and me west-seaxena witan to rihte
righted, that I they might let (be) so free so thiefs whether
gerehton, thæt ic hi mot lætan swa freo swa theorve swather
I will. And I for God's Love, and for my Soul's thrift,
ic wille. ac ic for godes lufan, and for minre sawle thearve
will, that they be their franchise worthy, and their [a] Courts.
wylle, that hy syn heora freolses wyrthe, and hyra Cyres.
And I in God's living Name bid that they no man nay
And ic on Godes lisiendes Naman beode thæt hy nan man ne
break, nay with fees manage, nor with not any thing, that
brocie, ne mid feos manunge, ne mid nænigum thingum, that
they not might choose such [b] man, such they will.
hy ne motan ceosan swulcne mann swylce hy wyllan.

And I will that man give them high-ones at Domerham
And ic wylle thæt man agyfe tham hiwum æt Domra-hamme
their Land [c] Book, and their [d] free-will such hand to choose,
hyra land bec, and hyra freols swulce hand to ceosenne,

[a] *Chairs* approximates nearer to the Original; hence the Chair of Justice, to take the Chair, to act as President.

[b] Patron, or Life Lord.—18 Liberi homines commendati tantum.
Little Domesday, for Norfolk, 249. a.

[c] Most probably Land-book or Book-land, since Alfred was not likely to have disseised them of that land, which Elfleda had conferred.

[d] We presume free-will or franchise, for it aproximates much nearer than the variation of spelling in many words—give for instance.

such

flæde. ⁊ for þa frýnd þe heo foreþingode. ⁊ ic foreþingie.

for me, and for Elfleda, and for the friends that ſhe did intercede for, and I do intercede for.

⁊ ſec man eac on cƿicum ceape ýmbe minre ſaple þearfe. ſƿa hit beon mæᵹe. ⁊ ſƿa hit eac ᵹerýſne ſý. ⁊ ſƿa ᵹe me forᵹýfan ƿýllan. *

And ſeek they alſo, with a living price, for my Soul's health, as it be may, and as it alſo fitting is; and as ye me to forgive ſhall be diſpoſed.

MANNING'S LATIN TRANSLATION.

* Item, Obteſtor, in Dei Nomine, et ejus Sanctorum, ut meorum conſanguineorum nemo, neque hæredum interpellet nemo, arbitrio ſuo utendi facultatem eorum quos redemi è ſervitute. Profecto mihi Weſt-Saxonum Optimates legitimum cenſuerunt, ut ego iſtos poſſem relinquere, ſive liberos, ſive ſervos, utrum vellem. At ego, propter Dei amorem, et propter animæ meæ ſalutem, volo ut ſint libertatis ſuæ compotes et arbitrii. Necnon in Dei viventis nomine obſecro, ut eos nemo vexet, neque pecuniæ exactione, neque alio quovis modo, quo minus poſſint eligere talem Dominum qualem ipſi velint.

Item, Volo ut reddantur familiis apud Domer Manerium, eorum Chartæ, et eorum licentia talem Dominum eligendi qualem ipſis placuerit, propter me, et propter Ælfledam, et propter amicos pro quibus ipſa intercedebat, atque ego intercedo.

Denique, Imploretur Deus, viventi pretio, pro animæ meæ ſalute, quantum fieri poſſit, uti etiam congruum eſt, et prout vos mihi condonare velitis.

ſuch them lieſeſt be, for me, and for Elfleda, and for the friend
ſwulce him leofaſt ſy, for me, and for Ælflæda, and for tha frynd
that hoo forethought and I forethink.
the heo forethingode and ic forethingie.

And ſeek man eke on [e] *wick* [f] *Cheap about my Soul's thriſt,*
And ſee man eac on cwicum ceape ymbe minre ſawle thearfe,
ſo it be may, and ſo it eke riſing be, and ſo yea me
ſwa hit beon mæge, and ſwa hit eac geryſne ſy, and ſwa ge me
forgiven (it) will.
forgyfan wyllan.

There are many other paſſages in this Will, that demand ſimilar Examination and Illuſtration. The Land which Alfred's Grandfather had entailed on the weaponed half, (that is) the Spear-half, in Oppoſition to the Spindle-half, and which, if transferred into a Wife's or Female Hand, he orders to be purchaſed by his Heirs, and reſtored to the proper Line, is conſtantly confounded with the Acquiſitions he had made, when the word is [g] aſtryndon, ſtrengthened, reſtrained, or ſtraitened, not begæton, as in the Introduction of this Record. In confirmation of this interpretation, we find him urging the juſtice of ſuch reſtoration of property to the entailed line, becauſe he had bequeathed to his Heirs Male, many more Eſtates than they would be neceſſitated to repurchaſe, that he might have beſtowed on Females. But we reſerve farther comment to a future opportunity, in our hiſtorical Diſſertation on Ranks and Services.

The next Specimen we ſhall exhibit is an antient Proclamation of Henry the third, which Somner conſiders a Saxon Record, Lord Lyttleton an Old-engliſh Document.—*Som. Dict. ad verbum unnan.*

[e] Alive—Northern Dialect—living—

[f] Cheap-men—modern Chap-men, ſelling their wares at a fixed *price.*

[g] For variation of ſpelling, take *give* an example—Giſ, yeſ, iſ, yſ, yeve, yeoven, given, giſſis, geive, gin ye will, gi' me.

ROTUL. PATEN. de Anno 43. Hen. 3. Memb. 15. Nº 40.

SOMNER ad verbum *unnan*.

Henr. þurg Godeſ fultume King [a] on Englene loande. Lhoaverd on Yrland. Duk on Norm. on Aquitain ⁊ Eorl on Aniou. ſend igreting to alle hiſe [b] holde ilærde ⁊ ilewed on Huntindonn ſchir. þæt ƿiten ge ƿe alle þæt ƿe ƿillen ⁊ unnen þæt þæt ure rædeſmen alle. oþer þe moare dæl of heom þæt beoþ ichoſen þurg uſ ⁊ þurg þæt loandeſ folk on ure kuneriche hebbeþ idon ⁊ ſchullen don in þe ƿorþneſſe of Gode ⁊ on ure treoƿþe for þe freme of þe loande. þurge þe beſigte of þan to foren iſeide rædeſmen beo ſtedefæſt and ileſtinde in alle þinge abutan ænde. And ƿe heaten alle ure treoƿe in þe treoƿþe þæt heo uſ ogen. ꝥ heo ſtede-fæſtliche healden ⁊ ſƿeren to healden ⁊ to ƿeren þe iſetneſſeſ þæt beon makede ⁊ beon to makien þurg þan to foren iſeide rædeſmen. oþer

Henricus Dei adjutorio Rex Angliæ, Dominus Hiberniæ, Dux Normanniæ, Aquitainæ, & Comes Andegaviæ, Salutem mittit (i. dicit) omnibus fidelibus ſuis, clericis & laicis in Comitatu Huntindoniæ. Vobis omnibus notum facimus, quod volumus & concedimus ut quod Conſiliarii noſtri omnes, ſive major eorum pars, qui fuerint electi à nobis & à gentis plebe in Regno noſtro, fecerint & facturi ſint (i. e. decreverint) in honorem Dei, & fidelitatis quâ nobis obligantur intuitu, pro bono gentis, per conſilium antedictorum conſiliariorum, (eo nomine ſcilicet) firmum ſit & ſtabile per omnia in perpetuum. Et præcepimus omnibus fidelibus noſtris, per fidem (vel, fidelitatem) quam nobis debent, ut firmiter obſervent & obſervare (vel, obſervaturos ſe) jurent & tueri, conſulta quæ ab antedictis Conſiliariis, ſive à majori ipſorum parte, facta &

[a] In Bibliotheca Aſſleianâ uniformly ou, not on.

[b] A different diviſion of Letters is adopted.

 ejuſdem

PATENT ROLL Anno 43. Henry 3. Memb. 15. N° 40.

Somner ad verbum *unnan*.

Henry through God's [a] *fultume, King of Englandsland,* [b] *Lord*
Henr. thurg Godes fultume, King ou Engleneloande, Lhoaverd
of Ireland, Duke of Normandy, of Aquitain, and Earl of Anjou,
ou Yrland, Duk ou Norman, ou Aquitain, and Earl ou Anjou,
send I greeting to all his whole [c] *servants of the Lord, and* [d] *allowed*
fend igretinge to alle hise hol theilaerde, and ilewede,
of Huntingdon Shire, that [e] *ween ye well all, that we will*
ou Huntendonn Schir, that witen ge well alle, thæt we willen
and wull, that that our [f] *Read-men all, or the more Deal of*
and [g] uune, thæt thæt our Rædesmen alle othe the moare Dael of
them, that be chosen thorough us, and thorough that [h] *Landsfolk,*
heom, that beoh ichofen thurg us, and thurg thæt Loandesfolk,

[a] Fultume, or Fulture, from Fultura, Support.

[b] Lif-erth—Life-earth—Source of Life or of Bread, *Loaf*, hence *Bread* is the *Stuff*, or *Staff*, of *Life*.

[c] From theow Servants, hence modern thief, and the Provincialifm, " Do you *thou* me, i. e. call me a flave ?"—in Lancafhire Dialect ftill theow.

[d] Allowed, lawful—Pacem Regis habentes in the Law—neither Villains or Thiefs—hence Alloy, or Allay—lawful Money with a proportion of lawful bafe Metal.

[e] The true Derivation of Words will fo eafily and naturally appear, from thefe Sources, that it will be frequently unneceffary to comment on them.

[f] Men of Letters—Reading—Witens—or Wifemen.

[g] Somner gives this Charter in his Dictionarium Saxonico-latino-anglicum, under the Verb unnan, a word no where found but in this paffage, according to his conception of the paffage.—The Original is abbreviated thus, wūne, and from the common expreffion in Lancafhire, " I will and wull," we have little doubt that our Interpretation is correct.——Lye is fubject to this error.

[h] The Folk of that County—Knights of that County—Communitas—for fimilar Writs were directed to each Shire of England and *Ireland*—Tyrrel's Common People is ridiculous, for there never was a Knight from an Irifh *Election*, a *Reprefentative* to an Englifh Parliament—but of this in our Hiftory.

in

þurȝ þe moare dæl of heom alsƿo alse hit is beforen iseid. And þæt æhc oþer helpe þæt for to done bi þam ilche oþe aȝenes alle men (paucula quædam hic deesse videntur, hæc scilicet aut similia: in alle þinge þæt) oȝt for to done ⁊ to foangen. And noan ne mine of loande ne of eȝteƿhær þurȝ þis besiȝte muȝe beon ilet oþer iƿersed on onie ƿise. And ȝif oni oþer onie cumen her onȝenes ƿe ƿillen ⁊ heaten þæt alle ure treoƿe heom healden deadlicheistan. And for þæt ƿe ƿillen þæt þis beo stedefæst ⁊ lestinde ƿe senden ȝeƿ þis ƿrit open iseined ƿiþ ure seel to halden amanges ȝeƿ ine hord. Ƿitnes us selven æt Lundæn. þane eȝtetenþe day on þe monþe of Octobr. in þe tƿo ⁊ foƿertiȝþe ȝeare of ure crunninge. And þis ƿes idon ætforen ure isƿoren redesmen Bonefac. archebischop on Kanterbur. Ƿalter of Cantelop bischop on Ƿirechestr. Sim. of Muntfort Eorl on Leirchestr. Ric. of Clar Eorl on Gloƿchestr. ⁊ on Hartford. Roger Bigod Eorl on

facienda sunt, sicut prædictum est. Et quod unusquisque, vigore ejusdem juramenti, contra omnes homines, in omnibus tum faciendis, tum recipiendis, ut id ita fiat & observetur, alter alteri sint auxilio. Et (quod) nullus sive de terrâ (vel, gente) meâ, sive quacunque aliâ, per consilium hujusmodi (hujus scil. consilii obeundi causâ) impediatur, sive damnum patiatur, ullo modo. Et si quis, sive vir sive fœmina, huic (edicto) contravenerit, volumus & mandamus ut omnes fideles nostri eos habeant infensissimos. Et quia volumus ut hoc firmum sit & stabile, mittimus vobis hoc scriptum patens, sigillo nostro signatum, penes vos in archivo reponendum. Teste nobis ipsis Londini decimo octavo die mensis Octobris anno coronationis nostræ (vel, regni nostri) quadragesimo secundo. Hoc autem gestum fuit coram juratis consiliariis nostris, Bonifacio, Archiepiscopo Cantuariensi, Waltero de Cantilupo, Episcopo Wigorniensi, Simone de Monteforti, Comite de Leicestrensi, Richardo de Clare, Comite Glocestrensi & Hartfordiensi,

in our King's Reach, haveth done and shall do, in the Worthi-
on ure Kyneriche habbeth idon and ſchullen don, in the Worth-
neſs of God, and in our Truth, for the Freemen of the Land,
neſſe of Gode, and on ure Treowthe, for the Freime of the Loande,
thorough the ſight of the heretofore ſaid Read-men, be ſtedfaſt
thurge the beſighte of thantsforen iſeide Rædeſmen, beo ſtedefæſt
and laſting, in all things without end. And we [i] ordain all our
and ileſtinde, in alle thinge abutan ænde. And we heaten alle ure
true (men) in the Truth that they us owe, that they ſteadfaſt-
treowe in the Treowthe thæt heo us ogen, thæt heo ſtede-fæſt-
like holden, and ſwearen to holden, and to warden, the [k] ſettineſſes
lich healden, and ſweren to healden, and to werien, the iſetneſſes
that bin maked and bin to make, thorough the heretofore ſaid
that beon maked and beon to makæn, thurg than to foren iſeide
Read-men, or thorough the more deal of them, alſo as it
rædeſmen, other thurg the moare dæl of heom, alſwo alſe hit
is beforſaid. And that each other help that for to do by their
is beforen iſeid. And thæt æhe other helpe thæt for to done bi them
[l] *ilk Oath, againſt all men right for to do, and to* [m] *fang. And*
ilche othe, agenes alle men rght for to done and to foangen. And
none nor of mine Land, nor of [n] *oughtwhere, thorough his ſetting*
noan ne mine of loande, nor of egte-whær, thurg his beſigte
may be lett, or worſed in any wiſe. And if [o] *ony or*
muge beon ilet, other iwerſed on onie wiſe. And gif oni other

[i] Higt, to command—Skinner—hence Engliſh ordain—heaten, a thing ordained.

[k] Setneſſes, things ſet at the Sitting, what was determined at the Sitting or Seſſions, ſynonimous to Aſſize Aſſia—Hence beheſt, be ſit, or ſet—what ordained at the Seſſion.

[l] Ilk, Spencer the *ſame.*

[m] Deſtruction ſang Mankind—Shakeſpeare, Timon.—We ſtill have Dogs-ſangs, Teeth, the Holders, conſequently hold.

[n] Anywhere—a Lancaſhire provincialiſm.

[o] Ony, Lancaſhire for any.—Here oni and onie are the maſculine and feminine gender, Man or Woman.

Norþfolk. ⁊ Marescal on Engle loand. Perres of Sauueẏe. Ƿill. of Fort Eorl on Aubem. Ioh. Plessiz Eorl on Ƿareƿik. Ioh. Geffrees sune. Perres of Munt-fort. Ric. of Greẏ. Roȝer of Mortemer. Iames of Aldiþel. ⁊ ætforen oþre moȝe.

diensi, Rogero Bigod, Comite Norfolciensi & Angliæ Marescallo, Petro de Sabaudia, Willielmo de Fort, Comite Albermarliæ, Johanne Plessiz, Comite Warwicensi, Johanne filio Galfridi, Petro de Monteforti, Richardo de Grey, Rogero de Mortuomari, Jacobo de Aldithel. & coram aliis pluribus.

And al on þo ilche ƿorden is isend into aurichte oþre schire ouer al þare kuneriche on Englene loand. ⁊ ek in tel Irelonde.

Et omnino eisdem (vel totidem) verbis missum est in unumquemque per universum regnum Angliæ Comitatum, ac etiam usque in *Hiberniam*.

CHRONICON

any come here againſt, we will and ordain that all our
onic cumen her ongenes, we willen and heaten thæt alle ure
truemen them holden [p] *deadly. If then, and for that we will*
treowe heom healden deadliche. If than, and for that we willen
that this be ſtedfaſt and laſting, we ſend you this Writ open
thæt this beo ſtedefeſte and leſtinde, we ſenden gew this writ open
ſigned with our Seal to hold amongſt you in [q] *Herd. Witneſs*
iſeined with ure ſeel to halden amanges gew ine hord. Witnes
ourſelves at London the eighteenth Day in the Month of
wi ſelven æt Lundæn thane egtetenthe Day on the Monthe of
October, in the two and fortieth year of our crowning. And
Octobr, in the two and fowertigthe geare of ure cruninge. And
this was done afore our ſworn Read-men Boniface Archbiſhop
this wes idon ætforen ure iſworen Rædeſmen Boneſac Archebiſchop
of Canterbury, Walter of Cantilupe Biſhop of Worceſter, Simon
on Canterbur, Walter of Cantelop Biſchop on Wirecheſtr, Sim.
of Montfort Earl of Leiceſter.
of Muntfort Eorld on Leircheſtr, &c.

The Saxon Poetry, that has been tranſmitted to us, admits of a ſimilar Tranſlation. The firſt ſpecimen we ſhall exhibit is the concluſion of a Saxon Ode on a Victory of King Athelſtan's. In this Poem Henry of Huntingdon complains of certain "*extraneous Words and uncommon Figures,*" which Warton terms "*Scaldic Expreſſions or Alluſions.*" We pretend not to any acquaintance with ſuch Language, but we are certain that he has not "given a literal Engliſh Tranſlation of this Poem," as he profeſſes. The Original is extracted from Gibſon's Saxon Chronicle, with his Latin, and Warton's Engliſh, Verſion.

[p] In the language of that age, wolf-headed, gerentes caput-lupinum.

[q] In Congregation—a Number aſſembled.

CHRONICON SAXONICUM.

Anno 938. [a] Gibſon. p. 114.

Ne ƿeaꞃð ƿæl maꞃe. on ðiꞅ eiᵹlanꝺe. æꝼeꞃ ᵹẏꞇa. ꝼolceꞅ ᵹe-ꝼẏlleꝺ. beꝼoꞃan þiꞅꞅum. ꞅƿeoꞃꝺeꞅ ecᵹum. þæꞅ þe uꞅ ꞅecᵹað bec. ealꝺe uðƿiꞇan. ꞅiððan eaꞅꞇan hiꝺeꞃ Enᵹle ⁊ Seaxe. up becomon. oꝼeꞃ bꞃẏmum bꞃaꝺ. Bꞃẏꞇene ꞅohꞇon. ƿlance ƿiᵹꞅmiðaꞅ. Ƿealleꞅ oꝼeꞃ-comon. eoꞃlaꞅ aꞃhƿaꞇe. eaꞃꝺ beᵹeaꞇan. [b]

Non fuit ſtrages major in hac Inſula unquam [plureſve] populi occiſi antehac gladii acie, (quos commemorant Liberi veterum Hiſtoricorum) ex quo ab Oriente huc Angli ac Saxones appellentes, & per mare latum Britanniam petentes, inſignes bellorum fabri, Britannos ſuperabant, Duces honore præſtantes: [&] terram occupabant.

[a] This Chronicle, edited by Gibſon, before he took his Maſter's Degree, approaches nearer to the Original, than any Verſion or Tranſlation we have met with. Gibſon was afterwards Biſhop of London;—He was a ſound Scholar, an able Divine, and zealous Friend to our Eſtabliſhment; he enforced pure practical Piety on true Chriſtian Principles, not for the grand *oſtentatious* ſake of "maintaining the Preeminence of our Church over all Proteſtant States," * he countenanced not Sectaries, he encouraged not Schiſmatics.

[b] "Never was ſo great a ſlaughter in this iſland, ſince the Angles and Saxons, the fierce beginners of war, coming hither from the eaſt, and ſeeking Britain through the wide ſea, overcame the Britons excelling in honour, and gained poſſeſſion of their land." See Diſſertation I. Warton's Poetry.

* See a late circular Letter—and occaſionally one Word, Sentence, or Action gives a truer Knowledge of the real Character, than the *Actor* diſplays on the Stage.—The benevolent, pious, and orthodox Charles Baldwin of Mancheſter, a lay Gentleman, but a ſound Divine, will probably enlarge on ſuch ſubject.

WARTON'S

SAXON CHRONICLE.

An. 938. Gibſon. p. 114.

[a] *Nor were there Wail more, in this Iſland, ever as yet, (with)*
Ne wærth wæl mare, on this Eiglande, æfer gyta,
folks filled, before this, (by) ſwords edges, thus they us
folces gefylled, beforan thiſſum, ſweordes ecgum, thæs the us
(that) ſeeketh book, elder oth' wiſemen, ſith-thence Eaſterns hither,
ſecgath bec, ealde uth witan, ſiththan eaſtan hider,
Angles and Saxons, up came, o'er (the) briny broad, Britain
Engle and Seaxe, up becomon, ofer brynum brad, Brytene
foughten, Lance with Smiths, Welch overcame, earls harrowed,
ſohton, wlance wig Smithas, Wealles ofer-comon, eorlas arhwate,
earth they gotten.
eard begeatan.

The numerous Extracts of antient Engliſh Poetry, publiſhed by Warton in the firſt Volume of his Hiſtory, are all copied from Originals in the Saxon Character, and chiefly tranſcribed from the Theſaurus of Hickes. We ſhall ſelect a Specimen, to prove the neceſſity of purifying the Text by conjectural Criticiſm, on rational principles, in this branch of Literature; and at the ſame time contradict that arrogant and ignorant aſſertion of the late Lord [b] Orford, that there "never did exiſt a more barbarous Jargon than the Dialect, ſtill venerated by Antiquaries, and called Saxon." Let us oppoſe "Jonſon's learned Soc," to this modern buſkin'd Hero. In [c] "Compoſition, our Engliſh Tongue, (which we think is

[a] They who are acquainted with Saxon Manuſcripts will juſtify this reading.

[b] Walpole's Hiſtoric Doubts, p. 10.

[c] Ben Jonſon's Engliſh Grammar, which we hope ſome ſound Scholar will ſpeedily reprint, with a few neceſſary alterations, to modernize it for the generality of readers. —To this Work Mr. Tooke is much indebted.

WARTON'S ENGLISH POETRY, Vol. I. p. 13.

Ƿƿhen ðꞃihꞇin o ꝺomeꞅðei ƿinð-
ƿeð hiꞅ hƿeaꞇe,
Anꝺ ƿeꞃpeð ƿæꞇ ꝺuꞅꞇi cheꝼ ꞇo
hellene heaꞇe,
Ƿe moꞇe beon a coꞃn i ᵹodeꞅ
ᵹulꝺene eꝺene,
Ðe ꞇuꞃꝺe ðiꞅ oꝼ laꞇin ꞇo Enᵹh-
ꞅche leꝺene
Anꝺ he ƿæꞇ heꞃ leaꝼꞇ onƿꞃaꞇ
ꞅƿa aꞅ he cuƿe. AMEN.

That is, " When the judge at Doomſday winnows his wheat and drives the duſty chaff into the heat of hell; may there be a corner in god's golden Eden for him who turned this book into [a] Latin, &c.

[a] This muſt ſolely be attributed to Warton's careleſſneſs, ſince, immediately preceding, he ſtates, " It was tranſlated from the Latin." The inaccuracy in the Saxon muſt be immediately obvious to the Scholar.

proved to be the Saxon) is above all other very hardy and happy, joining together, after a most eloquent manner, [d] *sundry words of every kind of speech.*"

[d] Selections from Jonson—Mill-horse, Lip-wise, Self-love, [*] Twy-light, thereabout, not-with-standing, † be-cause, Table-nap-kin, Wood-bind, a Puff-cheek, Draw-well, Handi-craft, Foot-ball-player, a Tennis-court-keeper ; we could subjoin innumerable other instances of its Precision, Accuracy, and Beauty, which entitle it to an Equality with the Grecian Language for combining Ideas, and fully establish its Superiority over the Latin and ‡ French vague Phrases and tautological Idioms. In || *Strength* and Simplicity it is unrivalled—only *two* Declensions of Nouns.

* Tween-light, betwixt Light and Darkness. † Be the Cause, or Case.

‡ I never see a Gallicism, or French Word anglicised, but I could exclaim with Ben Jonson's Peniboy—" There's a fine new Word Thom, pray God it signify any thing."

Staple of News.

|| Seven Consonants to one Vowel—the Sound an Eccho to the Sense.

WARTONS' ENGLISH POETRY, Vol. I. p. 13.

When [a] *Do-right o'* [b] *Dooms-day winnoweth his wheat,*
Hwhen drightin o domesdei windthreth his hweate,
And throweth the dusty Chaff to Hell's Heat,
And therweth thæt dusti Chef to hellen heate,
Ah! might be one Corner in God's golden Eden,
He mote be ona corn i godes guldene edene,
That throweth this of Latin to English [c] *reading,*
The turthe this of Latin to Englische redene,
An he that her least unthrowed so as he couth.
And he thæt her least onthrat swa as he cuth. Amen.

[a] The Title of our Lord.

[b] Doom Judgment—Wind-throweth—wind-thrath. Warton has mistaken the *th* for *w* thrice, and *p* for *w* once, in these five lines.

[c] In antient MS. the *r* approximates in form frequently to a *j* or *f*.

Warton prefaces his Work by a curious aſſertion that "the Saxon Poetry has no connection with the nature or purpoſe of his undertaking;" but if any reader will conſult Hickes's learned Theſaurus, he will find "moſt [d] Citations (not) extracted from ancient Manuſcript Poems never before printed," but verbatim et literatim tranſcribed from the Anglo-ſaxon printed characters, without amendment, or alteration, in the diviſion or explanation of the Original. We ſhall exhibit one Extract to facilitate the reading of ſuch Poetry, in Warton's Language, and our correſponding modern, accented, and divided rythmically.

Màiden Margaret—one Night in priſon lay,
Meiden Margarete one nitt in priſon lai,
Hèr came before Olibrius—on that other Day.
Ho com biforn Olibrius on that other dai.
Màiden Margaret—liſt up upon my Lay,
Meiden Margarete, lef up upon my lay,
And Jeſu thou believeſt on—thou do him all away.
And Ihu that thou leveſt on, thou do him al awey.
Live in me and be my Wife—full wèll thou may ſpeed,
Lef on me ant be my wife, ful wel the mai ſpede.
Antioch and Aſia—ſhalt thou have to meed:
Auntioge and Aſie ſcaltou han to mede:
Check-lawn and purple Pall—ſhalt thou have to wed:
Ciculauton and purpel pall ſcaltou have to wede:
With all the Meàts òf my Lànd—full well I ſhall thee ſeed.
With all the metes of my lond ful vel I ſcal the fede.

[d] Preface, p. 6.

The

The accomplished Alfred, in his valuable Translation of Bede's Ecclesiastical History, has transmitted a Chorus, or Burthen of a Hymn, of the presumedly inspired Cædmon. The judgment of this Monarch would not permit him to imitate Bede's affected Version, and he consequently transcribed the Original. Any Scholar that will compare the venerable Author's [a] sense of this passage, or collate the various Readings of different Manuscripts of this Poem, will make great allowance for our imperfections; for we pretend not to be uniformly right, though, we imagine, less incorrect than our predecessors. We give our Original from the best Edition.

EXTRACT from BEDE'S [b] HISTORY, and a FRAGMENT of CÆDMON. Smith's Edit. p. 597, and 170.

Cædmon sing me somewhat, then answereth he and quoth, not
Cedmon sing me hwæt, tha andswareth he and cwæth, ne
can I none thing sing, and I for-that of this Boroughship
con ic nan thing singan, and ic forthon of thyssum gebeorscipe
[c] *outed and hither* [d] *gowed, for that I naught sing nay couth. After*
uteode and hider gewat, forthon ic noght singan ne cuth. Eft
him quoth he, that with him speaking was, However thou might
he cwæte se, the mid him sprecende wæs, hwæthere thu meaht
me sing, quoth he. What shall I sing, quoth he. Sing me
me singan, cwæth he. Hwæt sceal ic singan, cwæth he. Sing me

[a] Hic est *Sensus*, non autem Ordo ipse Verborum.
Bed. Ecclef. Hist. Edit. Smith. p. 171.

[b] We have taken the privilege of adopting such Readings as we judge the purest, and of modernizing some words.

[c] Went out.

[d] Modern went.

BEDÆ ECCLESIASTICA HISTORIA cum FRAGMENTO CÆDMON. Ed. Smith, p. 579 & 170.

Cedmon. sing me [hƿæt] hƿegu. ða ⁊sƿaredý he ⁊ cƿæþ. Ne con ic nan ðing singan. ⁊ ic forþon of ðýssum gebeorscipe ut eode ⁊ hider geƿat. forþon ic noht [singan ne] cuþe: Eft he cƿæþ seþe [mid] him sprecende ƿæs. Hƿæþere ðu meaht me singan. cƿæþ he. Hƿæt sceal ic singan. cƿæþ he. Sing me frumsceaft: þa he ða ðas ⁊sƿare onfeng. ða ongan he sona singan in herenesse Godes scýppendes ða fers ⁊ ða ƿord ðe he næfre ne gehýrde. ðara endebýrdnesse ðis is.

Cædmon, inquit, canta mihi aliquid. At ille respondens, Nescio, inquit, cantare; nam & ideo de convivio egressus huc secessi, quia cantare non poteram. Rursum ille qui cum eo loquebatur, Attamen, ait, mihi cantare habes. Quid, inquit, debeo cantare? At ille, Canta, inquit, principium creaturarum. Quo accepto responso, statim ipse cœpit cantare in laudem Dei conditoris versus, quos nunquam audierat, quorum iste est sensus:

Nu ƿe sceolan herigean heofon rices ƿeard. metodes mihte ⁊ his mod geþanc. [ƿeorc] ƿuldor fæder. Sƿa he ƿuldres gehƿæs ece Drihten ord onstealde. he ærest gescop eorþan bearnum heofon to rofe halig scýppend. ða middan geard mon cýnnes ƿeard ece Drihtne æfter teode firum foldan frea ælmihtig.

Nunc laudare debemus auctorem regni cælestis, potentiam creatoris, & consilium illius facta Patris gloriæ. Quomodo ille cum sit æternus Deus, omnium miraculorum auctor exstitit, qui primo filiis hominum cælum pro culmine tecti, de hinc terram custos humani generis omnipotens creavit.

[e] *forming of Creatures. When he then this answer* [f] *unfanged,*
frumſceaert [g] Tha he tha thas andſware onfeng,
then began he ſoon ſing in earneſt, God ſhaping (it), that
tha ongan he ſona ſingan in herenеſſe, Godes ſcyppendes, tha
verſe and that word, that he never nay heard —their end-burthens
fers and tha word, the he næfre ne gehyrde—thara endeburdneſſe
this is.
this is.

Now we ſhall hearen [h] *heaven's* [i] *Reach word, mighty's might;*
Nu we ſceolan herigean heofon Rices weard, mitodes miht;
and his mode of thought; worked worlds father; ſo he worlds
and his mod gethanc; weorc wuldor fæder; ſwa he wuldres
give was; eke Do-right earth in ſtilled; [k] *he erſt ſhaped* [l] *elder*
geh wæs; ece Drighten ord onſtealde; he ereſt geſcop ælda
Barns [m] *Heavens to roof holy Shaping; then middle earth*
bearnum heofon to rofe halig Scyppend. tha middan geard
men's kind [n] *world eke Do-right after tied,* [o] *free folds from*
mon cynnes weard ece Drihtne æfter teode, ſiram foldan frea
(*the*) *Almighty.*
Ælmihtig.

[e] From frm, on our ſyſtem, are derived firm, form, from, farm, formation, &c.

[f] Unfanged—oppoſite to fang—not-hold—let go—delivered.

[g] The Saxon ꝼ and ƿ are eaſily miſtaken.

[h] The concluding n the antient characteriſtic of the plural number, as loven, choſen, &c. became obſolete in the time of Henry the eighth, and in the opinion of Ben Jonſon this change has produced great confuſion and errors in our language.

[i] Synonimous with Realm.

[k] The Father.

[l] M. S. Eliens.

[m] To Heaven's Roof.

[n] The omiſſion of a letter here, l, is ſometimes not to be much regarded.

[o] Men created free beings.

The

The numerous errors of Wheloc, the quondam Arabic and Saxon Cambridge Profeſſor, have been ſo fully proved by the ſubſequent Editor of Beda, that it might appear unneceſſary to give any Extract from his Works: but ſince he has attempted to tranſlate part of a curious old Engliſh Poem into Latin Verſe, we will juſt exhibit a Specimen.

BEDÆ ECCLES. HIS. PER WHELOC, p. 25.

Poeta quidam noſtras & vetus. M.S. Coll. Trin. Cantab. p. 10, ita cecinit.

of all for one Woman
...... of alle for one Wiman
That Helen was yclejed this Battle firſt began;
That Heleine was icleped this Baitaille firſt began;
One high man was there before, that yclejed was Dardan,
On heig man was ther bifore, that ycleped was Dardan,
Of him come the good Brutus, that was the firſt man,
On him com the Gode Brutus, that was the furſte man,
That Lord was in England, as I you tell can.
That Louerd was in Engelond, aſe ic eu telle kan.

Sic Latinè dedi—hæc unica fœmina, prima.

Ante omnes *ſævit* Trojani *ſemina* Belli
Hanc *Britones* dixere Helenam, *ſed* Dardanus ille
Excelſus Bruti pater extitit, unde Britanni
Heroum ſumpſere genus; fortiſſimus idem
Hunc *orbem* primus regere & dominarier anſus.

 Having

Having proved the inadequacy of all our beſt Saxon Scholars to convey accurate ideas of the [a] "Britiſh-ſaxon, Anglo-ſaxon, or Norman-ſaxon Documents," through the medium of a [b] Latin Tranſlation; and having, as we preſume, ſhewn that the Engliſh Tongue is the natural offspring of theſe Languages, (and Children ſurely have more Affinity to their Parents, and are better acquainted with them, than Aliens,) we will make an Extract from the Goſpel of St. John, to manifeſt the ſound Divinity in the Verſion edited by Junius, and then briefly ſuggeſt ſome Hints to Students relative to the beſt mode of cultivating the Knowledge of ſuch Literature.

The GOSPEL of St. JOHN. Chap. I.

1. On ꝼꞃuman ƿæꞅ ƿoꞃd. ⁊ ꝥ ƿoꞃd ƿæꞅ mid Gode. and Gode ƿæꞅ ꝥ ƿoꞃd.

2. Ðæt ƿæꞅ on ꝼꞃuman mid Gode.

3. Ealle þinᵹ ƿæꞃon ᵹeƿoꞃhte þuꞃh hẏne. ⁊ nan þinᵹ næꞅ ᵹeƿoꞃht butan hẏm ðæt ᵹeƿoꞃht ƿæꞅ.

4. On him ƿæꞅ liꝼ. and ðæt liꝼ ƿæꞅ manna leoht.

1\. *In* [c] *forming was* [d] *Worth, and the Worth was* [e] *midſt God,*
1\. On fruman wæs word, and the word wæs mid Gode,
and God was the Worth.
and Gode wæs the word.

[a] Such are the artificial Diviſions of the Moderns. Warton's Eng. Poetry.

[b] All the beautiful Preciſion of our Language is loſt in their Terms. How is the definite Saxon meaning of ᵹeheꞃꞅumneꞅꞅe, *here ſummnings*, that is, Lanfranc's attempt to make the Archbiſhop of York ſwear to obey the Summons of the See of Canterbury, deſtroyed by Gibſon's obſequium. Sax. Chron. p. 175.—or Wheloc's profeſſionem.

[c] Forming or firming, i. e. the Creation, or Eſtabliſhment of things.

[d] There is no Article, conſequently, it cannot with propriety be rendered Word, and what a train of thought does Worth ſuggeſt—firſt as Goodneſs or Excellence—then as Price—the Price of Man's Redemption.

[e] It may be of no great conſequence whether *midſt* or *with*, but when we conſider the Omnipotence of the Almighty, the former conveys a ſublime idea.

2. *That was in forming midst God.*
2. Thæt wæs on frumen mid Gode.
3. *All things were wrought thorough him, and not one thing*
3. Ealle thing wæron geworhte thurh him, and nan thing
not was wrought be-out him, that wrought was.
næs geworht butan hym, thæt geworht wæs.
4. *In him was Life, and that Life was man's Light.*
4. On him wæs Lif, and thæt Lif wæs manna Leoht.

There never was an Heresiarch, that displays not his want of common sense and judgment, when he attempts to pervert the Doctrine contained in these simple and sublime Verses, whether Arius, Crellius, or Gilbert Wakefield. The Translation of the fourth verse by the last, in his lately edited English Testament, surpasses, if possible, in absurdity, the whimsies of all his predecessors. " What was made had Life in it, and this Life was the Light of Men." That is, what was itself created, was the Cause of Creation to all created Beings, " All things were wrought thorough him." But as controversial Divinity is not our immediate Subject, we shall cease farther comment; though we take this opportunity of noticing, that in the twelfth Verse of this Chapter, where our English Translation renders, " to them gave he power to become the *Sons* of God," the Saxon Version has, " he sealed them one [c] would, that they were God's *Barns*," he ꞅealde him anpealð ꝥ hi pæꞃon Goꞇeꞅ beaꞃn. *Children*, not *Sons*, as the learned Dr. Vincent observed to me, that the Original is τέκνα Θεȣ, not υἱοι, for the term " Sons" tends to confound our ideas of the Trinity in this Chapter.—But to resume our immediate object,

The attentive reader must have observed, that the same Saxon word is frequently spelt in a different manner even in a few lines;

[c] Would—Power—I would, could, should, &c. Lily's Grammar.

and that in our Rendering we have almost totally disregarded the [f] Vowels. We have certainly adopted such system, and we find it to answer far beyond our expectation; not only in the interpretation of Saxon Records, but in appropriating the Scite of Places in the celebrated Book of Domesday. We might more rationally expect classical spelling in a modern Country-fellow, than an uniform mode of writing in our Saxon Ancestors, and we must investigate the meaning of each in the same manner. To this Principle another must be subjoined, that is, the Distinction of Words that have an [g] affinity to each other in sound, or that are pronounced by the same organ, and which are often substituted for each other. The Hebrew Division of Letters will here assist us, that is, their Discrimination into those pronounced by the Tongue, Lips, Palate, Teeth, Throat, or such as are of the serpentine description, or hissing letters. We must farther note the Syllables that are lost in modern pronunciation, as ge, a, in the beginning of Words, um, un, on, an, n, es, &c. at the end: and also not much regard changing an *m* into a *nu*, or *nn*, and vice versa with each respectively, a p into þ, or ƿ into p, when the sense demands such alteration; because the latter have frequently been mistook for each other, and the first in antient Manuscripts cannot be distinguished. The Specimens we have exhibited will teach more than any instructions we can suggest by *certain* Rules, but we strongly recommend, to the Saxon Student, the actual pronunciation of every word that appears unintelligible to him, and to place particular emphasis on the Consonants. Without pursuing some such plan, it never would have been discovered that [h] Belicolt, Bilesolt, Bilissolt, Briccode, Berisout, Beriscolt, were intended to

[f] This mode is now uniformly adopted by Scholars in the Hebrew Language, and Dr. Vincent is of opinion that the Greek Consonants are principally to be relied on.

[g] d and t.

[h] See my Specimens and Parts of the History of South Britain.

designate

designate the same Hundred, Byrcholt, in Kent; or that Seward, Osward, Sewart, Sidgar, Sigar, Siret, distinguished the celebrated Earl of Northumberland; or account for Turbatus being changed into Robertus, in less than three lines.

We will now attempt to sketch out a new Mode of studying Saxon Literature. Mr. Tooke is certainly correct in stating that "[1] our Ancestors were ignorant of the false Divisions and Definitions

[1] Diversions of Purley, p. 325.—This Author has certainly great merit, but he assumes more than he is entitled to; he says that "except in *if* and *but* (in one sense of the word) I believe all former Etymologists are against me." Vol. I. p. 146. What does he say to anan, grant—onleʒan—dimittere, hoc dimisso, eac, eacan, augere, to add, *Skinner*—ʒet, ʒeta, yet *Lye*—along—*on lang*. Also, alʒ—Bote, remedy *bi-utan*, bi-innan—be out, be in—*Tyrwhit*—and *Hoogeven* first suggested the idea to him, that all Particles were originally Verbs or Nouns.——There is so much extraneous matter in this publication, and he so constantly "seizes every impertinent opportunity of insult *," talks of being "confined without the most flimsy pretence," and has conducted himself in such an † inflammatory manner on the Hustings at Covent-garden; that I am stimulated to record a circumstance, omitted in the short-hand Report of his Trial, and which may perhaps a little ‡ embitter his life.——

"Does Mr. Tooke recollect one afternoon at the Old Bailey, about five o'clock, "when the Attorney-General had retired from Court for refreshment, and the Soli- "citor-General was examining Evidence relative to the Proceedings of the Scotch "Convention?—Does Mr. Tooke recollect rising indignantly, and wondering how "such Evidence could implicate him?—Does Mr. Tooke recollect stating, that he "certainly was in the Chair when the two first Resolutions of the Constitutional So-

* This applied to T. Warton, p. 90.

† Such as this to his rabble——"Gentlemen,—Ministers, last year, made you eat Bread with all the Bran in it, this year (if you will let them) they will make you eat Bread made of Bran only——Next year (if you submit to it) they will make you eat Bread made of Bran with chopt Straw in it——Gentlemen—If you will follow my advice, eat nothing but fine white Bread, made of the finest wheaten Flour, and then Ministers will take care you shall have it."——This stated by an intelligent man, who must have known, that Government, by their Bounty on Importation, had reduced Wheat six shillings per Bushel in a few weeks. To such conduct I cannot help exclaiming,

"That man I hate, as ill as hell,
"Who this can think, and that can tell."

‡ Whilst I have my life, it will never be embittered for any regret for the past. P. 230.

"ciety,

nitions fince received." Later Writers, by adopting the Diftinctions of Greek and Latin Grammarians, have confounded our Language and deftroyed its fimplicity. The Diverfions of Purley contain much ufeful information to the Saxon and Englifh Student, and fupply fome excellent elementary Rules. As a Scholar, the Author of "Επεα Πτεροεντα is entitled to our refpect; as a Member of Society, we pity his fiend-like mind, " whofe fole intent is ever to do ill." But the [k] Effence of this huge work, now extending to three quarto volumes, and exceeding the German [l] Hoogeven in bulk, on the Particles of a Language, might have been comprized in fifty pages. Indeed a *Horn-book*, conftructed on a fimilar principle to the one hundred and thirty-fifth page of his work, would contain the fubftance, though not the proofs.

" ciety, approving of their conduct, were carried, but that he then retired, and Mr. " Gerald occupied it?—Does Mr. Tooke recollect his artful infinuation to the Jury, " that it was natural to prefume that he withdrew in difguft, becaufe he did not ap- " prove of the fubfequent Refolutions? &c. &c.—And does he recollect that when " Sir John Scott was fent for into Court—that Sir J. inftantly handed a paper to " Mr. Woodfall?—Does he recollect that Mr. Woodfall fwore that it was Mr. " Tooke's hand-writing?—Does he recollect that this paper contained *every* Refo- " lution paffed at fuch Meeting, approving of the Proceedings of the Scotch Con- " vention?—Does Mr. Tooke recollect covering his face with his hand, finking into " his chair and exclaiming, " AND A FEW COPIES UNFORTUNATELY PRINTED?" —Does Mr. Tooke recollect that he could not again lift up his head that evening?— In your own language to Mr. Windham—" Thou has fac't many things,—thou could not face this!"——Such is the acquitted guiltlefs innocent.——Thefe things I heard and faw. S. H.——And whatever opinion Judges may have delivered, I ever fhall be of the fame fentiment with that found Lawyer Sir John Scott, that not one iota of the Evidence of the Bifhop of Gloucefter, who had no connection or intercourfe with Mr. Tooke twenty years preceding his Trial, could in the leaft excriminate this Arch-jacobin's actions, for the laft five years—though old women, like pigs, " can " fee where other folks are blind."

[k] The Quotations are generally frivolous; he ftill reads Greek Authors, through French Tranflations; and when *triumphing* over the ingenious Harris, an excellent Grecian, and boafting of " Authorities in his Favour, if you pleafe Mr. Harris's favourite Authority," (Greek) gives a flimfy French Tranflation of Plutarch. P. 283.

[l] Hoogeven de Græcis Particulis, 2 vols. 4to.

The reader muſt long have obſerved, that we conſider the Learning of Hickes, in his Anglo-ſaxon Grammar miſemployed; and the Introduction to Lye's Dictionary of little authority. Indeed we are convinced, that they have increaſed the difficulty of acquiring a knowledge of this language. For in our native tongue there are only two variations of the Subſtantive's Termination, into s, the mark of the concurrence of two Nouns, or the ſign of the Plural Number, as [m] Land-ſcapes, Self-freedom's Love; which in combination is frequently omitted, for we might ſay Self-freedom-love, as Self-love; or an addition of en, another mode of forming the Plural, as Ox, Oxen; or a change of the Vowel, as Man, Men, in the Saxon generally um, as Man, Mannum, Maniȝ, Moneȝum.

The conſtruction of the Verb is the moſt ſimple and eaſy, that can be found in any language. There are only two Inflections in the active Verb, the preſent, and the paſt, *do*, *did*. With the aſſiſtance of theſe two ſimple Actives, and other Verbs, equally ſimple, yet ſignificant, every complex variation of the Greek, or Latin, can be clearly expreſſed. We will exemplify this from the Latin, premiſing, that, originally, when an idea of the preſent was intended to be conveyed, our forefathers pronounced the d ſoft, th—ðo, when the paſt, hard, do, did—*Preſent* Singular, I love. or do love, thou love-in-is, or loveneſt, by abbreviation loveſt, and loves,—he love-do or loveth. Plural, we [n] love-in, ye love-in, they love-in. *Paſt*—I love did, by contraction lovedd, written loved. *Paſt* and *preſent joined*, with the aſſiſtance of the Verb *have*. I

[m] Land-ſhape.

[n] In Love—from the Saxon on, the act of loving. Ben Jonſon ſays, The perſons plural were wont to be formed by adding en, (ſoftened from in,) thus loven, ſayen, complainen, but now, whatſoever is the cauſe, (one will be ſuggeſted) it hath quite grown out of uſe, and that other ſo generally prevailed, that I dare not preſume to ſet this afoot again: Albeit (to tell you my opinion) I am perſuaded that the lack hereof, well conſidered, will be found a great blemiſh to our Tongue. Jonſon's Gram. *Since this Book is not eaſily found, it may be proper to note, that it begins at page 670 of his Works in Folio, though omitted in the Catalogue of Contents.*

have

have loveth, or d, that is, I have love do, or been in the act of loving, and continue to love. *The conditional past*, I had loveth, or ð, that is, I had love do, or been in love, if such a circumstance had not occurred. *The future* is expressed by the Verbs will and shall, whose various significations give our language a manifest superiority over the Greek and Latin. What is termed the commanding Mood, is expressed with peculiar energy and propriety—first, love thou, that is, þeop, love slave; then by the assistance of many Verbs, as *let* him love, *permit* him to love, *suffer* him to love, *allow* him to love, *grant* him to love, he *shall* love. In the Moods generally termed *Optative*, *Potential*, and *Subjunctive*, our language has an astonishing pre-eminence and wonderful precision. We can use God *grant*, *give*, *cause*, *permit*, &c. [o] may might, [p] can could, shall should, will would, owe ought, which with do as th, and did dd, and the Verbs *is*, *are*, *was*, *have*, &c. will convey more accurate ideas, than any language in the world. What has been termed the Infinitive Mood, and always been written *to love*, should be, we believe, *do love*, that is, be in the act of loving—*do hear*, to be in the act of hearing, probably written to, that distinction might be made betwixt the indefinite do hear, and when a Pronoun is prefixed, I do hear.—Doth is formed from *do* doubled *do-do*, a Provincialism in many counties. Love-ing, Participle from love-in, the act of love-ing. For *of loving*, *in loving*, &c. we refer to Επεα Πτεροεντα.

In what is termed the passive Voice PRESENT, (i. e.) loveth, *I am loved by* RIGHT-WISE *men*, converse, *righteous men love do me*. PAST, *I was loved or lovedd by time-serving-men*, converse, "*time-serving-men did love me*." Have, had, will, be, been, &c. will explain the rest, when the distinction betwixt *do* ð, and did ðð hard,

[o] Originally mæᵹ, past, maᵹbiðen, hence, probably, the mæᵹ, those who have power, which is translated Kinsmen.

[p] Can—can diden, in the plural originally then coulden, l, a letter half-vowelish, according to B. Jonson.

is underſtood. The Paſt completed in ſome Verbs, as taken, broken, was, we think, originally, take-end, break-end; but when the pronunciation, in the time of Henry the Eighth, had ſoftened theſe to taken, broken, it then became neceſſary, for diſtinction's ſake, to drop the final n plural. On the ſame principle done, do-end, in the northern counties it is ſtill pronounced as do-ant—ſpoken, ſpoke-end. Indeed our ſlow-ſpeaking anceſtors always annexed ideas, or common ſenſe, to their words, and this nation, happily, has retained the language that can convey them; but the Norman and French innovators, " talking like popinjays," have ſo apoſtrophized, abbreviated, or cut ſhort our Mother Tongue, to give volubility to *their tongue*, that labour and penetration are neceſſary to diſcover the Parent-Root from the altered Form of the Off-ſpring. But Prudence commands me to deſiſt, for [q] Experience has convinced

[q] This Eſſay has been written ſubſequent to the publication of my Specimens and Parts of the Hiſtory of South Britain; the ſecond number of which I am prepared to ſend to the preſs inſtantly; but I certainly will not injure myſelf by the expence of engraving Maps, nor print one ſyllable, till I have two hundred Subſcribers. No money is paid till the delivery.—And here I take leave to let a Right Honourable genealogical-loving Preſident again *hear* from me. At the requeſt of an antiquarian Friend, I ſent my Specimens of the Hiſtory of South Britain to this exalted Character. A month ſubſequent I called in Groſvenor-ſquare for this Nobleman's opinion, and left my card. In a few days I was informed by the Porter, that his Lord knew no ſuch perſon, but if I had any buſineſs I might ſignify it by a Letter. I wrote as reſpectful an Epiſtle as I could indite. I called again, and again, and again, and again. At laſt the Lacquey informed me, that it required no anſwer. Seeing no neceſſity why the Inſulter ſhould keep my Book, I wrote ſtating, that as my Specimens were of no value to him, I would thank him to return it by the Porter.—I called for it again and again. No anſwer. I then apprehended that the Letters might not have been delivered, for want of a proper fee. In conſequence I again wrote to this Noble F. R. S. &c. ſtating theſe circumſtances, and my ſuſpicions, and gave him ſtill an opportunity of examining it. It was then ſent to Mr. Faulder, either from his Lordſhip or his ſervant, with, " Let me hear no more from him."—Such is the patronage received from the Preſident of a learned Body, incorporated for antient Reſearch, the Subject of my Work—Or ſuch the raſcality of Porters.—I am not an F. S. A ——There are other literary and exalted characters of a ſimilar deſcription.

me,

me, that, in general, the prefent age is fond only of frivolous inveftigation.

To the Saxon Students, efpecially the junior Members of the Univerfity of Oxford, and thofe particularly from the northern fide of the Trent, we take leave to fuggeft a few brief obfervations on the mode of cultivating a knowledge of the Anglo-faxon language. When thoroughly acquainted with the characters, and capable of eafily difcriminating betwixt þ an p, ꝛ and ɲ, confider ð and þ or even ƀ as of the fame power, and m, n, u, as frequently requiring reciprocal changing, from the blundering of tranfcribers. (After reading this Effay with fome little attention,) begin with the Saxon Gofpel of St. John, without any Tranflation, and pronounce the Confonants of each word diftinctly, that is not underftood. In long words attend principally to the ftrong Confonants r, s, n, d, or þ in the centre; for this language, like the Hebrew, has numerous prefixes and fuffixes, and a perfon fkilled in the pronunciation of that tongue, will derive great advantage from fuch circumftance. To the Greek Scholar we recommend the plan, on which Scapula's Lexicon is formed. Firft find the Root, as frm—from whence we have [1] forme, form, from, frame, firm, all implying a Beginning, then firmed, whence farmed, fecured to the Tenant on fuch conditions—and thence farm—farmer—and its dependancies—its modern affixes, affirm, confirm, and fuffixes, firmnefs [2], &c. Thus from the Stream with which we are acquainted we may trace the Source, and derive fatisfaction from the inveftigation. If a correfponding word does not immediately occur to the mind, we may frequently recur with benefit to Skinner, the Gloffary of Chaucer, the Hiftory of Englifh Poetry by Warton, Spenfer, Douglas, our

[1] Adam our forme Father—Chaucer—Mr. Tooke's from—beginning.

[2] *Nefs*, when ufed in Topography, implies uniformly a Curvature, from the Latin Nafus, our nofe, nefs; annexed to other words it correfponds with *[illegible]*, and may be borrowed from Neft, or the Seat, or Refidence of that Quality it is coupled with. We ftill fay *Neft of Robbers.*

antient Chroniclers, black-lettered Characters, and for the last resource to Lye; but he certainly pays too much attention to Vowels. The Dictionary of Johnson may often be resorted to with great advantage, for antique or classical authorities, and the sense affixed to the word by different Writers; for though we are convinced that his Etymologies are little to be depended upon, the Work is certainly not a [t] " disgrace to the Nation," or to the Author; his Collection from the Antients has been of great use to the man who abuses him, and his gigantic mind could never be exercised fruitlessly. He certainly has done more for Literature, for Happiness, for Virtue, than that self-consequential Snarler, the venomous [u] Viper of Democracy, once well-nigh strangled by our herculean Monarch, and whose hissings, and forked tongue, dare not now so openly threaten the Royal abode.

An acquaintance with the Lancashire Dialect of Mr. Collier will greatly facilitate the reading of Saxon Authors, and his short Glossary may be of some service, though his pretended distinctions of the derivations from Saxon, Belgic, Dutch, or British, are to be totally disregarded. We have selected a few Words from his Dialogue, which certainly displays original Humour, where the Consonants correspond nearly with our modern Terms, at least in Power or Sound, and which may serve to elucidate the original Derivation and confirm our system—*arnt*, Errand, rnt, or run it—*Beawt*, Mr. Tooke's be-out—*blend it*, be-laid it—*awlung*, all-along, Mr. Tooke's along—*staw*, stand all, all at a stand—stangs, sittings, whereon they sat—*donn*, do-on—*doff*, do-off—*fair-faw*,

[t] The petulant Mr. Tooke's assertion, who terms his own Enquiry about the Conjunctions, Prepositions, and Adverbs of our Language his " *Diversions*."——What are his grand literary pursuits, or *grand objects*, that he only occasionally *deviates* from ?

[u] Mr. Tooke knows the metaphor, who is allied to that sibilant Race

—— —— —— whose forked Tongues
Are steept in Venom, as their Hearts in Gall.

Ben Jonson's Speech of Envy.

 fair-fall,

fair-fall, or fair happen it unto—*faigh*, saw, connecting sight and see—*shiar*, share, Division, modern shire—*greadly*, go rightly—*ogreath*, on-go-right—*lack-o-day*, ah-luck-o 'th day—and we have some Consonants that convey the same Idea with every Vowel, *clack*, *cleck*, *click*, *clock*, *cluck*—the Note of our domestic Fowl to her Brood.—This mode of study will occasionally require great exertions of the mind, but it will ultimately be attended with more certainty and satisfaction.

The Scholar will soon find, that the Saxon radical words are in general monosyllables, and that most of the terms in our language, (the [x] richest, most copious, and definite in the universe) convey a distinct meaning, if that meaning could be discovered. Thus Spinster is placed in opposition to Wife. Search for the distinction —wif—wives—weave, wove, west, woof—spindle-stir, (i. e.) move —Spindster, modern Spinster—Hence we obtain information that the Matrons superintended the Loom, the Virgins the Spinning of the Wool. The word [y] Lady in a similar manner conveys an Idea,

[x] This the learned Michaelis allows.—See Prize Dissertation on the Influence of Opinions on Language and of Language on Opinions, p. 36.—And here I cannot omit the compliment to our nation by this general Scholar, " the false ornaments of the French language are never more striking, than on comparing them with the beautiful Simplicity of English Writers, who seem to mind only things."

Translation, p. 68.

[y] At the fest of Estre tho Kyng send ys sonde
That heo comen alle to London, the hey men of this Londe
And the Lovedys al so god, to ys noble fest wyde
For he schulde crowne here, for the hye tyde.

Warton. Vol. I. p. 53.

MODERN ENGLISH, with nearly the same CONSONANTS in SOUND.

At the feast of Easter—the King sent his * Command
That they come all to London—the high men of this Land
And the Ladies all so good—to this noble feast hied
For he should crown there—for the high tide.

* Sent his *send*, or sonde, corrupted by Latin Scholars to *summoned*, s, and c, easily changed in Pronunciation—Command.

the

the beloved. The whole of our Mother Language, we entertain little doubt, will admit of ſimilar illuſtration ; and if a few ſound Scholars, well verſed in Engliſh Literature, would thus dedicate a few months attention to the cultivation of Saxon Learning, there is little queſtion, but we ſhould ſpeedily obtain, not only a Grammar ſuperior to thoſe of Lowth, and Jonſon ; not only a Saxon Lexicon, on the principle of Scapula, with Engliſh Notes and Illuſtrations, but a Dictionary, not indeed more voluminous; though far more valuable, than that of our late reſpectable, learned, laborious, and conſcientious Lexicographer. The literary object to which we have pledged ourſelves, if ſupported, is of no leſs moment ; but ſhould we be diſcouraged, that ſtudy, perhaps, may be continued by us at ſome future period, which at preſent we only pretend to have cultivated ſubſerviently to a faithful Knowledge, of our antient Britiſh Hiſtory.

THE END.

www.ingramcontent.com/pod-product-compliance
Lightning Source LLC
Chambersburg PA
CBHW022025080426
42733CB00007B/726

* 9 7 8 3 3 3 7 2 0 9 7 6 6 *